Dynamic Discipleship

Paul W. Powell

BROADMAN PRESS
Nashville, Tennessee

All Scripture quotations, unless otherwise indicated, are from the King James Version.

All Scripture quotations marked RSV are from the Revised Standard Version of the Bible, copyrighted 1946, 1952, ©1971, 1973.

All Scripture quotations marked NASB are from the New American Standard Bible. Copyright © The Lockman Foundation, 1960, 1962, 1963, 1971, 1972, 1973, 1975. Used by permission.

Dewey Decimal Classification: 248.4
Subject Heading: DISCIPLESHIP
Library of Congress Catalog Number: 84-11388

Library of Congress Cataloging in Publication Data

Powell, Paul W.
  Dynamic discipleship.

  1. Christian life—Baptist authors.   I. Title.
BV4501.2.P5964   1984   248.4'861   84-11388
ISBN 0-8054-5004-1 (pbk.)

Dedication

To *Charles Moore,* a faithful friend
To *Alan Johnson,* a helper in time of need
To *Joe Barentine,* a brother and builder of churches

Foreword

For more than a quarter of a century, Paul W. Powell has been doing the work of a pastor—and doing it uncommonly well. During those years, he has been a treasured friend and often a confidant in the gospel ministry. I first knew Paul as a neighboring pastor and fellow student in a car pool. As some of you may know, in that car pool we hammered out our theology on the way to and from the seminary classroom.

Very early Dr. Powell demonstrated gifts as a diligent student, pastor, and preacher. Through the years he has stayed at the task. This book, *Dynamic Discipleship,* is the fruit of his life and ministry.

Paul is himself a believer who continues to grow. He both proclaims his faith and lives it. He combines a high seriousness about the lordship of Christ with a contagious, wholesome sense of humor.

As a pastor, God has used him to evangelize, disciple, nurture, and lead those under his shepherding care. Green Acres Baptist Church, where he serves, is a model of pastoral care and oversight where discipleship has a high priority.

Paul believes that preaching makes a difference. He is uniquely gifted as a communicator with a fine balance between biblical exposition and practical application. He preaches to win, to instruct, to inspire, indeed to change lives by the power of God's Word.

Because he is widely used in conferences and conventions, some would consider him a "preacher's preacher." However, his greatest strength is his pastoral preaching. This book grows out of such a ministry to his own people.

When you read this book you will profit from several positive elements in every chapter, such as:

- solid biblical interpretation,
- touch of reality in daily life,
- centrality of Jesus Christ as Lord,
- the significance of church fellowship,
- the basic disciplines of discipleship, and
- the struggle in the journey.

This volume comes from the life of a believer to believers. It can be reliable as a tool, a guide, an encourager, a leaning post, a prod, and a light for the journey. I am honored to commend to you *Dynamic Discipleship* and its author, my friend Paul Powell.

LLOYD ELDER, *President*
Baptist Sunday School Board

Introduction

Michelangelo, as a boy, presented himself to a master sculptor to be his pupil. The old man said, "This will take all your life." Michelangelo replied, "What else is life for?"

With such submission to the Savior we should give ourselves to being his disciples. *Disciple* is a relationship word. It refers to one who is so closely related to Jesus that he not only wants to learn his teachings and obey them, but he wants to become like him. A disciple is one who is so personally committed to Christ that she is willing to give up her very life for him if necessary.

The making of disciples is Jesus' primary interest. Just before his ascension he said, "All authority in heaven and on earth has been given to me. Go therefore and make disciples of all nations, baptizing them in the name of the Father and of the Son and of the Holy Spirit, teaching them to observe all that I have commanded you; and lo, I am with you always, even to the end of the age" (Matt. 28:18-20, RSV).

Most of us have been taught that the command of this Great Commission is "go ye therefore." The verb forms used in the passage, however, give us a different picture. The only command in the statement is to make disciples. The other action words are present participles, which actually mean "as you are going, baptizing and teaching, make disciples." Discipleship is the final result he seeks; the other things are to that end.

The appeal of this book is that we first become disciples ourselves, and then that we give ourselves to developing other believers into real disciples.

If you decide to do this, it will take all your life. But what else is life for?

Contents

Dynamic Discipleship

1. The Three Dimensions of Discipleship

The word *disciple* is the Holy Spirit's favorite word to describe the followers of Christ. In the Gospels and the Book of Acts, it is used over 270 times to describe believers. Technically, the word *disciple* means "a student" or "a learner." It describes a person who submits to the instruction and the authority of another. Practically speaking, the word *disciple* is a synonym for a Christian. Luke writes that the disciples were first called Christians at Antioch (Acts 11:26*b*).

In the Christian sense then, a disciple is a person who has accepted Jesus Christ as his Lord and Savior and is seeking to learn from, obey, and follow after him as the Master of his life.

Being a disciple of Jesus is a decisive and a demanding decision that begins a new life for a person. Jesus clearly taught his would-be followers that allegiance to him must take precedence over all other ties. A person may have to give up his occupation, friendly relations with parents and kin, or even life itself to fulfill the demands of discipleship. The way of Christ led him to rejection, suffering, and death; it may become the way of these things for us also. Jesus cautions us not even to consider becoming his disciple until this cost had been clearly counted (Luke 14:25-33).

What is involved in discipleship? What are the marks of a true follower of Christ? If you are considering becoming a disciple of Jesus, you need to know what you are getting into. Discipleship as set out by Jesus is three dimensional.

He tells us that it involves obedience to God, love for our brothers, and witnessing to the lost world (John 8:31; 13:34-35; 15:8). Three words sum up the heart of discipleship. They are the words *faithful, fellowship,* and *fruitful.*

Commitment and Continuation

The first characteristic of a disciple is faithfulness. Jesus said, "If you continue in my word, then are ye my disciples indeed" (John 8:31). A disciple then is one who on a daily basis continues in the word of God.

Becoming a disciple is much like getting married. It is relatively easy to get married. In fact, if you were to ask me to perform your wedding ceremony, I would tell you exactly where to stand, what to say, and everything to do. And my record time for a wedding ceremony is seven minutes flat! But you know that there is more to marriage than a wedding ceremony. You do not make a fluttering vow to your husband or wife and then promptly forget the relationship. Marriage is a commitment followed by a continuing relationship. Discipleship is the same way. It involves coming to Christ as Savior and Lord and then continuing in his Word daily.

Becoming a disciple is also much like becoming a parent. It takes a relatively short period of time to have a baby. A few months of pregnancy, a few hours of labor, and the baby is born. But there is more to parenting than conception, pregnancy, and birth. Being an effective parent is a continuing relationship and responsibility. It goes on as long as you live.

A lady was in the hospital to give birth to her first baby. As the labor pains became more frequent and severe, she gasped to the nurse, "Is the hard part about over?" The nurse replied, "Honey, this is the easy part. The hard part will last for the next eighteen years."

Becoming a disciple is the same way. It is relatively easy

to receive Christ and to be born again; but thereafter, you are to continue in his Word as long as you live. Being a disciple is an act of commitment followed by a lifetime of continuing.

What does it mean to continue in Jesus' Word? It means that on a daily basis we learn and live the Word of God. The aim of Bible study is not primarily to build up a reservoir of knowledge so that we can impress people with how much we know. Its purpose is that we might be conformed to the image of his Son. The purpose of Bible study then is not to fill our heads but to change our lives.

Continuing in God's Word was one of the things that characterized the early Christians. Luke described the New Testament church following Pentecost in this way, "Then they that gladly received his word were baptized: and the same day there were added unto them about three thousand souls. And they continued stedfastly in the apostles' doctrine" (Acts 2:41-42). The apostles' doctrine and the teaching of Jesus are the same thing. The apostles were preaching about who Jesus was, what Jesus did, and what he had said. To continue in their doctrine was to continue in his Word.

All of us have a certain life-style. Behind that life-style is our value system or our philosophy of life. Our values or our philosophies determines the clothes we wear, how long our hair is, our actions, and our attitudes in life. There are only two sources for our value system: from human sources or from God. Disciples are persons who gets their values from what God says in the Scriptures.

Many people who claim to be disciples are more influenced by what people say than by what God says. Through television, books, magazines, and the daily newspaper, they are repeatedly exposed to human value systems, and these are the influences that most affect their actions and attitudes. What we need is to learn God's value system and to live it in our daily lives.

The other day I was driving down the street listening to my radio. I keep my radio set on the "easy-listening" music station in our town. I pulled up next to a young man who had the volume on his car stereo turned up so high that I could hear it through both of our car windows. His whole car seemed to be vibrating with the rhythm of the music. When I looked at him he was bouncing up and down and twisting around. He looked for all the world like he might be having a seizure. Why was he acting one way, and why was I acting another way? It was because we were tuned in on different stations. The music we were listening to was affecting the actions of both of us. I was cool and calm, and he was alive and jiving.

It is the same way in the spiritual realm. What we are tuned in on spiritually affects our whole lives. A disciple is a person who daily tunes in to the apostles' teachings—to Jesus' Word—and lets them determine his values and his actions.

If you are not learning and living God's Word on a daily basis, you can't really call yourself a disciple. You should never let a day go by without spending some time in Bible study. A disciple is a person who faithfully continues in God's Word.

Holding Hands with One Another

The second mark of discipleship is fellowship. I do not use the word *fellowship* in the traditional sense of a church party with cookies and Kool-Aid. I use it in the New Testament sense of caring for and sharing with one another. Jesus said, "A new commandment I give to you, that you love one another; even as I have loved you, that you also love one another. By this all men will know that you are my disciples, if you have love for one another" (John 13:34-35, RSV).

There are no soloists in the kingdom of God. To be a

disciple of Christ is to choose to hold hands with other Christians. It is to become a part of the body of Christ. If we are all members of his body, then when one member is honored we are all honored. And when one member of the body suffers, we all suffer. One person can't hurt without the rest of us hurting. One person can't rejoice without the rest of us being happy. To be a disciple involves a commitment of love to the body of Christ (1 Cor. 12:13-27).

What is love in the Christian sense? Christian love is active, willing, caring. It is a commitment of our will to what is best for someone else.

I can determine to hate, ignore, or love anyone I so choose. All three of these actions are actions of the will. I choose to do them or not to do them. I am not a helpless victim of either of the emotions: hate, indifference, or love. I do as I want to.

My commitment to love others does not mean that I have to agree with them. Two people can be brothers without being identical twins. We do not have to see eye to eye in order to walk hand in hand.

It doesn't even mean that I have to like them—in the sense that I approve of what they do or even enjoy being with them. As Christians we are enjoined to love people whether we like them or not. The best illustration of loving persons without liking them that I know of is the way we feel about ourselves. We do not always like ourselves, but we do always love ourselves. If other people don't like everything I do, I can surely understand that. I don't even like everything I do myself. But in spite of that, I love myself.

Human nature leads most of us to limit our love to those who are like us. We like people who generally reflect our values and attitudes. Anyone vastly different from us is usually not one of our favorite people.

In every church I have pastored, there have been people

I didn't particularly like. Usually, they were people who were different from me, so I didn't enjoy being around them. However, even though I didn't like them, I loved them. I did everything I could to help them. When they called me, I was as quick to go to their aid as I was to go to the aid of my best friend. Not liking them did not keep me from loving them and seeking what was best for them.

The real achievement of Christian love is in loving the unloved and the unlovely. As Christians we recognize that there is a concern demanded of us by Jesus which makes liking people irrelevant.

A disciple then is someone who has a love relationship and a commitment to love all people—especially other Christians. In fact, John tells us that we are to lay down our lives for the brethren (1 John 3:16). You say, "I can't do that. I don't love other people that much." I'm glad you have discovered that. The high demand of discipleship can not be met in our own strength. Only as we are drawn to God through Christ can we experience the power to love the unlovely as he did (John 6:44*ff.*). People with all of their limitations can seldom give heartfelt affection to one another. Natural dislikes, cultural prejudices, personal wounds—all prevent the full flow of creature love. But by the power of God, people can desire good even for those who do them ill; they can act with love and justice toward others for whom they may feel no concern. A disciple is a person who is continually learning how to be like Christ. He has not attained; he is not perfected, but he is learning, and he is loving.

How Good Is Your Cotton?

The third mark of a disciple is fruitfulness. Jesus said, "By this my father is glorified, that you bear much fruit, and so prove to be my disciples" (John 15:8, RSV).

The fruit Jesus refers to here is introducing other people

to Christ. It is the fruit of evangelism. It is sharing Christ with others. Jesus made this clear when he said later, "Ye have not chosen me, but I have chosen you, and ordained you, that ye should go and bring forth fruit" (John 15:16). Notice that word *go*. Obviously, Jesus is not talking about the fruit of the Spirit. To develop love, joy, peace, long-suffering, gentleness, goodness, faith, meekness, and temperance, you do not need to go anywhere. You could live in a monastery and develop much of that fruit. But if you are going to bear the fruit of evangelism, you must go.

There are four factors in producing fruit. First, one must have good seeds. Without seeds all agriculture comes to a halt. Second, one must have productive soil. One can't raise a crop on the Rock of Gibraltar. Third, one must have the right season. It takes a warm climate for a crop to grow. And, fourth, there must be a sower. Even if one has good seed, productive soil, and a warm climate, it is to no avail unless someone sows the seed.

The same four factors are important in producing spiritual fruit. In the parable of the soil Jesus taught us that the seed is the gospel, the soil is the human heart, and we are the sowers. If we will busy ourselves at sowing the gospel seed in human hearts in a warm and loving manner, we will see much fruit from our lives.

One day several cotton farmers were whiling away a winter afternoon around a potbellied stove. They soon became entangled in a heated discussion on the merits of their respective religions. The eldest of the farmers had been sitting quietly, just listening, when the group turned to him and demanded, "Who is right, old Jim? Which one of these religions is the right one?"

"Well," said Jim thoughtfully, "you know there are three ways to get from here to the cotton gin. You can go right over the big hill. That's shorter, but it is a powerful climb. You can go around the east side of the hill. That's not too far, but the road is rougher'n tarnation. Or, you can go around the west side of the hill which is the longest way but the easiest.

"But, you know," he said, looking them squarely in the eye, "when you get there, the gin man don't ask you how you come. He just asks, 'Man, how good is your cotton?' "

Old Jim was right, you know. When we as disciples stand before the Lord on judgment day, he is not going to ask, "How did you come? Did you come the Methodist way? Did you come the Presbyterian way? Or did you come the Baptist way?" I think what he will want to know is: "How good is your fruit?"

Let me bring all of this into focus with just one question, "If you died today, is there anyone who could look into your casket and say of you, 'Thank God, I'm a Christian because of you.' " Is there anyone that you have led to Christ, or is there anyone who will meet you in heaven and say, "You are responsible for my being here"?

Some unknown poet wrote about a friend:

> When she enters the beautiful city,
> And the saved all around her appear,
> Many people around will tell her,
> It was you who invited me here.

Could that be said of you? It should be if you are a real disciple.

What does it mean to follow Jesus? Who or what is a disciple? A disciple is a person who is committed to Jesus Christ in such a way that she continues in God's Word on a daily basis; she has a love commitment to the body of Christ, the church; and she is witnessing and sharing Christ with other people.

Dietrich Bonhoeffer was a great Christian if there ever was one. Even though it cost him his life, he would neither yield to Hitler's lies nor run from Hitler's power. While many German Christians who did not believe in Hitler's Nazism left the country, Bonhoeffer did not. He said: "I will not have the right to preach to my people when the war is over if I do not suffer with them through it." So he spent the last years of his life in Hitler's concentration camps. He became a symbol of courage to other Christians. They loved and praised him. Much of their praise got back to him.

Out of that great man's Christian heart came some statements which have encouraged me more than anything I have read outside the Word of God. He spoke of knowing himself to appear confident to others yet full of fear in his heart. The last lines of his long discourse state: "Who am I? They mock me, these lonely questions of mine. Whoever I am, thou knowest, O God, I am thine!"

That's what a disciple is. He or she is a person who belongs to Jesus Christ heart, mind, body, and soul.

2. More Like the Master

Perhaps the most important question in life for every one of us is this, "When you get where you are going, where will you be?" Everybody is going somewhere. So, what is your goal? What is the purpose of your existence? Why are you here on earth?

As a disciple of Jesus Christ, you need to know where you are going. You need to have the goal of discipleship clearly in mind. If you don't, your life will lack the direction and the discipline that ought to characterize dynamic discipleship.

What is the goal of Christian discipleship? It is not to get off the road to hell and eventually to arrive in heaven. It is that we grow to "a perfect man, unto the measure of the stature of the fulness of Christ" (Eph. 4:13).

The Greek word translated *perfect* is *teleios.* It means to be mature, fully grown, or whole. It does not suggest sinlessness. This word was sometimes used to describe a sacrifice that was fit to be offered upon the altar. At other times, it was used to describe a fully grown man in contrast to a boy who was just a lad. And it was used at times to describe a student who had become proficient in a subject in contrast to one who was just a beginner. Or it sometimes described a tool that was suited for a particular need.

Let's suppose that I needed a screwdriver to repair my lawn mower, and I asked you to bring me one. After you handed it to me you might ask, "How is that one?" And I would say, "It's perfect." I wouldn't mean that the screwdriver was flawless. I would simply mean that it was the right size for what I needed at the time. The goal of the Christian life is that we might be perfect in the sense that we measure up to everything God wants us to be. It is that we become mature men and women spiritually. As someone has said, "You don't have to be perfect today, but you should have perfection as your goal tomorrow."

Having identified the goal of discipleship, Paul then personifies it. He shows us the goal in flesh and blood. We are to grow unto "the stature of the fulness of Christ."

Charles Howard, a well-known Baptist preacher, once told of taking a group of children to a nursing home to sing for its elderly residents. As they sang the song "More Like the Master" he heard one of the children singing unfamiliar words. So he listened carefully to catch what they were. Instead of singing "More like the Master I would ever be," a little boy was singing, "More like the pastor I would ever be."

The pastor, of course, should be like the Master. But so should every other Christian.

The word *fullness* refers to all the qualities that made Jesus what he was. Jesus is the one perfect, fully mature person who has lived on the earth. He is the standard by which all Christians should be measured. No other standard is adequate. No other offers the continuous challenge that he offers. He is the one person who reveals absolute maturity. He walked as every man should walk. He talked as every man should talk. He lived as every man should live. He loved as every man should love. He trusted as every man should trust God. In his actions, his attitudes, and his approaches to life, he showed complete maturity in every way.

The ambition of many Christians seems to be just to get by. They are busy going to church but not growing in Christ. They want to make a creditable showing, to be reasonably good, to keep from falling into flagrant sin, to have religious respectability, and above all, when life's day is done, to land safely in heaven. But that's all. Beyond that they seemd to be content. Most disciples today seem to be geared to mediocrity rather than maturity.

If being like Christ, if full Christian maturity is the goal of discipleship, if we are to be conformed to his likeness, then we need to know what Jesus was like. Unless we know what he was like, then we cannot know what we are to become.

It is difficult of course to sum up the life of Jesus in just a few words. But there are four marks of maturity readily seen in the life of Jesus and set out in the Bible. These qualities in his life helped to make him the perfect person he was. If we are to be mature, these qualities must be in our lives also. These four marks of maturity are compassion (Matt. 9:36), control (Jas. 3:2), confidence (Jas. 1:3-4), and commitment (Phil. 3:13-15).

A Friend of Sinners

The first mark of maturity readily seen in the life of Jesus is his love for and his acceptance of all people. One of the things for which Jesus was most severely criticized by the religious establishment of his day was that he welcomed sinners as his friends and even went so far as to eat with them. In fact, all people including foreigners, tax collectors, moral failures, and social outcasts found a friend in Jesus. He even loved, forgave, and prayed for his enemies.

The story of the woman taken in the act of adultery beautifully depicts how Jesus treated people (John 8:1-11). The Pharisees caught a woman in the very act of immorality. They brought her to Jesus and reminded him that the law of Moses said that she should be stoned to death. They wanted to know what he thought they should do. This was all an attempt to publicly discredit Jesus, for this law of Moses had long since fallen into disuse.

Jesus staggered them by saying, "He that is without sin among you, let him first cast a stone at her" (v. 7). Then he stooped down and began to write in the dirt. When he looked up, the woman's accusers had all slipped away. Their hearts had condemned them of their own sins, so they left. Then Jesus asked the woman where her accusers were, and she replied that they were all gone. Jesus then said to her, "Neither do I condemn thee: go, and sin no more" (v. 11).

This experience reveals three ways we can deal with sin and sinners. We can stone them as Moses did. We can expose them and embarrass them as the scribes and Pharisees did. Or we can forgive them as Jesus did.

Don't get the idea that Jesus condoned or coddled sin. Jesus didn't pat this woman on the shoulder and say, "Honey, it's OK. Don't worry about it, it really doesn't matter all that much." He called her act what it was: sin. He didn't condone her act, but neither did he condemn her. He forgave her and told her to go and live a life of chastity from that day forward.

This kind of love for others, especially the unlovely and the unloving, is a mark of spiritual maturity. It characterized the life of Jesus, and it should characterize the lives of all of his followers.

Jesus taught us that we should be perfect (*teleios*) as our Father in heaven is perfect (Matt. 5:43-48). This involves in part treating our enemies the same way that God treats his enemies. How does God treat his enemies? He treats them with the same kindness and generosity as he does his friends. When God's sun shines, he lets it shine on those who curse him as well as on those who praise him. And when God sends the rains, he lets them fall on the farms of those who reject him as well as on those who accept him. God acts as benevolently toward the atheist as he does toward the believer.

It is natural to treat your friends kindly. It is normal to

speak to those who speak to you. But it is Godlike to love your enemies, to praise those who curse you, to do good to those who hate you, and to pray for those who persecute you.

If we are going to be like our Heavenly Father, then we must learn to love our enemies as we love our neighbors. A love for all people, especially for their enemies, characterizes both God and Christ. If we are going to be more like the Master, then we must learn to love other people unconditionally as he loved them.

Hold Your Tongue

Another thing that characterized the life of Jesus was his complete self-control. At all times and under all circumstances, Jesus lived a disciplined life. This is never more evident than during the experiences that surrounded his trial and crucifixion.

There has probably never been a more illegal trial in all of history than the trial of Jesus. The Jewish leaders violated their own laws in at least nine different ways in their efforts to get Jesus condemned. His trial was a kangaroo court from the beginning to the end. These religious leaders wanted Jesus dead, and they didn't care what they had to do to accomplish that purpose.

But with all of these obvious injustices, Jesus maintained a dignified silence and a masterful self-control. He controlled both his tongue and his temper, his actions and his reactions.

The apostle Peter holds up Christ's conduct during all of this unjust treatment as an example for us today. He said that Christ "did no sin, neither was guile found in his mouth: Who, when he was reviled, reviled not again; when he suffered, he threatened not; but committed himself to him that judgeth righteously" (1 Pet. 2:22-23). Jesus trusted God so much that he feared no man. And he could take injustice without retaliation because of his confidence in God.

This kind of self-control is a mark of spiritual maturity that should be found in the life of every disciple. The apostle James taught us that self-control is one of the primary marks of spiritual maturity. He said, "For in many things we offend all. If any man offend not in word, the same is a perfect [*teleios*] man, and able also to bridle the whole body" (Jas. 3:2).

The tongue is a very small part of our body, but it exerts tremendous power for good and for evil. And it is the hardest thing in all of life to control. If a person can control his tongue, he then has the maturity and discipline to control the rest of his life also.

Think of all the sins that are committed with the tongue: blasphemy, profanity, lying, nagging, gossip, complaining, and criticism.

Do you have trouble controlling your tongue? If you do, you probably have trouble controlling your thoughts and your temper, your time, your attitudes, your appetites, and your actions. But if you can control your tongue, you can probably also control these other areas of your life.

The person who can control his life is a mature person. Such self-control characterizes the life of Jesus, and if we are to be more like the Master self-control must characterize us.

Trust God in Everything

Jesus walked among men with an absolute confidence in God. When he stood before Pilate who had the power of life and death over him, Jesus said, "Thou couldest have no power at all against me, except it were given thee from above" (John 19:11). Though he was misquoted, misunderstood, falsely accused, and beaten beyond recognition by the public officials of his day, his spirit was unconquerable, and his attitude was always positive. He knew that God was at work in his life, and nothing could destroy that confidence in God.

This kind of confidence in God is a mark of maturity. Nothing shows our spiritual maturity quite as much as our response to trials and difficulties in life. James taught us that trials are a part of God's perfecting (*teleios*) process (Jas. 1:2). They are a means by which God teaches us and refines us as he attempts to mature us.

While we do not believe that everything that happens to us is willed directly or intentionally by God, we do believe that at least all things are permitted by him. Nothing ever happens or touches our lives that does not first pass under his Fatherly eyes and through his loving hands. This means that an experience may appear to be evil and full of destructive implications; but nonetheless, if God allows it, he will bring something good out of it. So, what ultimately matters in life is not what happens "to" us but what happens "in" us.

Life is tough, and our spirits are so easily beaten down by the circumstances around us. But if we have the spiritual maturity of Christ Jesus, then we know that even out of the bad things of life God can bring some good. In fact, God often uses the bad and the sad things to conform us to the image of his Son Jesus (Rom. 8:28-29).

This kind of confidence is a mark of spiritual maturity. It characterizes the life of Jesus, and if we are to be more like the Master it must characterize our lives also.

Facing Jerusalem

The final thing that marked the maturity of Jesus was a wholehearted commitment to the will of God. He was committed to doing the will of God at all costs. Nothing, and no one, could distract him from this commitment. Though he knew that the cross awaited him, still he set his face like a flint toward Jerusalem (Mark 8:31). This was the will of God and he was committed to it at all costs.

This attitude of mind, this absolute commitment to the achieving of God's will, is one of the marks of spiritual maturity. It also characterized the apostle Paul. Paul freely admitted that he had not yet achieved full Christian maturity. He was far from what he ought to be. Nevertheless, he said that he was pressing on to become everything God wanted him to be. The single-minded commitment of his life was to achieve the will of God also. Then he wrote, "Let us therefore, as many as be perfect [*teleios*], be thus minded" (Phil. 3:13-15).

All spiritually mature people have this same attitude. They are so committed to doing what God wants that they will not let anybody or anything distract them. Someone asked the keeper of the cemetery, "What are the two most common epitaphs found in the cemetery." He replied, "They are 'Rest in peace,' and 'Thy will be done.' " Isn't it sad that the will of God is so often associated with tragedy and death. The Bible declares that the will of God is the finest thing that could ever happen to any one of us.

The will of God gives life a sense of completeness, and it satisfies the deepest longings of the human heart (Rom. 12:2).

A wholehearted commitment to God's will characterized the life of Jesus, and if we are to be more like the Master it must characterize our lives also.

To be like the Master is the goal of discipleship. God wants to leave the imprint of his Son Jesus Christ on your life and on mine. I have read a great deal about the so-called shroud of Turin. In the cathedral of Turin in north Italy, there is a herringbone fabric that has on it the image of a crucified man some think to be the image of our Lord. Some say that this is just a medieval hoax by clever artists. Others say that it is demonic in its origin. Some scientists have said they believe that it is really the image of the Lord.

I do not know about the shroud of Turin. But I can assure you of this: the intention of God is not to leave the image of his Son on a piece of medieval cloth; it is to leave the image of his Son on your life and on my life. He wants us to become like Jesus Christ, the only fully mature person who ever lived. This is the goal of Christian discipleship. Don't stop short of it.

3. Counting the Cost

Jim Fiebig said, "When someone demands blind obedience, you'd be a fool not to peek." He is exactly right. Commitment without counting the cost can be catastrophic.

Surprisingly, Jesus never called anyone to blind obedience. On the contrary, he demanded that people who became his disciples be fully aware of all that was involved before they committed themselves to him. He wanted no blind allegiance. He wanted disciples who would follow him with eyes wide open.

Again and again, Jesus would pause in his teachings to remind the crowds of the cost of discipleship. So careful was Jesus about this that no person could ever accuse him of misrepresenting his cause or his call. Luke gives us an example of this in his Gospel (Luke 14:25-35). The occasion for this teaching was a time of immense popularity for Jesus. The masses were thronging to him. Crowds always worried Jesus. He knew that many of the people would be swept along by emotion or follow him simply because others did. He knew they were not serious enough in their commitment.

Moreover, he had just told the parable of the great supper. It was the story of a man who gave a great feast. The man represented God, and the supper represented salvation and all of its ramifications. The host invited many people to be a part of this great event. But when all the preparations were made, those who had been previously invited made all kinds of excuses as to why they could not come.

The master was clearly upset. So he sent his servants out very quickly into the streets and the lanes of the city to invite the poor, the crippled, and the blind to come to his great supper. The servants returned with the report that many had accepted the invitation, but that there was still room for others. So the master sent them out a third time. This time he told them to go down the highways and the farm-to-market roads and to urge everyone they saw to come to the supper. The point of this parable is that no one is excluded from God's offer. It is an unlimited invitation. It is extended to all men. But lest people should think that because his invitation is unlimited it is also unconditional, Jesus pauses to set out the demands of discipleship.

A careful reading of this statement of the cost of discipleship reveals that the phrase "he cannot be my disciple" is repeated three times. It is found in verse 26, verse 27, and verse 33. In each instance, it is preceded by one of the demands of discipleship.

We cannot read such strong statements as these without a sense of uneasiness. This call of Christ is a constant reminder to us that while salvation is free, it is not cheap. It challenges us to give our highest and our best devotion to him. We cannot, he says, be his disciples unless we are willing to subordinate every other relationship under him, suffer any hardship for him, and surrender all ownership to him.

What is the cost of discipleship? What demands does Jesus place on us? They are clearly set out here. He demands unrivaled love, unreserved commitment, and unrestrained sacrifice.

Unrivaled Love

The first demand Jesus makes is that of supreme loyalty. He says, "If any one comes to me and does not hate his own father and mother and wife and children and brothers and sisters, yes, and even his own life, he cannot be my disciple" (v. 26, RSV). The word *hate* is a troublesome word. When we read it we think, "Wait a minute, Lord, my wife? My parents? My children? You can't mean that. Didn't you say that we should honor our father and mother? Don't the Scriptures teach that husbands should love their wives? How then can he demand that we "hate" our nearest and dearest loved ones before we can be his disciples?" That word *hate* staggers us.

That's exactly what it is intended to do. It is an Aramaic word which literally means "to love less." It does not mean that we are to despise, look down upon, or reject our family. It does mean, however, that we are to love Christ more than we love them. It means that the claims of Christ are to be above and before every other claim in our life. Our relationship to him is to come before every other relationship. We are to give to him the supreme loyalty of our life. It means that in comparison to every other person on earth, Jesus must be number one to us. There are to be no rivals to our loyalty to him. We must not love anyone else more than Christ or put anyone else before him.

Jesus is dealing with the competitions of life. He names those rivals, those loyalties, that so easily compete with his call for our allegiance. And he does not name the low things of life that compete with him. He names the higher ones. Jesus had no lack of appreciation for the family. He taught loyalty and devotion to one's family. And our family can be a great support to us as we serve the Savior. But natural affection is not to come between you and the Lord. Your family can also put pressure on you and distract you from Jesus. They can be hostile toward Jesus, create conflict in your heart, and actually compete with him for your loyalty. If the time ever comes when you must choose between Christ and your mother or father, wife or children, brothers or sisters, you must choose loyalty to him. He comes first. He demands that.

In her book *My Memories of Ike,* Mamie Eisenhower tells that one of the reasons why General Dwight D. Eisenhower was such a great leader and had such ability to inspire others was partly due to his deep love and loyalty for his country. She said, "I learned early in our married life about his single-minded devotion to America." She said that in their first home, an apartment near Fort Sam Houston in San Antonio, Texas, he kept his gear packed and ready for action at all times. After they had been married only a month, Ike was given a new assignment and announced to Mamie that he must leave her for the time being. She said to him, "Ike, you are not going to leave me this soon after our wedding day, are you?" He put his arms around her and said gently, "Mamie, there is one thing you must understand. My country comes first and always will; you come second."

Mamie said it was quite a shocker for a nineteen-year-old bride who had been married only one month to hear, "You come second."

That's the way it must be with the true disciple of Jesus. If the time ever comes when a choice must be made, the true disciple must say kindly but firmly, "Honey, as much as I love you there is one thing you must understand, Christ comes first and always will; you come second." If you aren't willing to say that, you cannot be a disciple of Jesus. He demands that kind of supreme loyalty.

Fortunately, in our country we do not often have to choose between our Savior and our family. However, in other countries that is often precisely the choice. I preached in an evangelistic crusade on the island of Trinidad in the West Indies several years ago. I found myself for the first time preaching to Hindus and Buddhists. Missionary Gayle Hogg helped me to understand that when I called on these people to follow Christ, I was calling upon them not only to give up their sins but at the same time to give up their families. That's exactly what it cost them to be a disciple of Jesus. And if they were not willing to pay that price they could not follow him. The same is also true for us.

Unreserved Commitment

The second demand that Jesus makes is that of absolute commitment. He says, "Whoever does not bear his own cross and come after me, cannot be my disciple" (v. 27, RSV). To most people today, the Cross is an ornament of beauty to be worn as jewelry around the neck or to decorate the steeple of a church. But in Jesus' day it was an implement of death. It was the Roman means of capital punishment. Those who heard Jesus that day had seen scores of people crucified on crosses as an open and public display of the consequences of disobedience to Roman law. The cross then meant one thing: death.

Jesus here uses the cross, not to show the price of disobedience to Rome, but to show what might be the price of obedience to God. He says that we must not only be willing to give up our family but also our lives if we are to be his disciples. We must be willing, if necessary, to bear the shame, hostility, and suffering of death if we are to follow him.

The desire for self-preservation is one of the strongest impulses in us. But even that must not come before our devotion to Jesus.

Then Jesus tells two brief stories to illustrate a point. He tells the story of a man who started to build a house without first sitting down and computing the cost of it. The results were that when he was half finished he ran out of capital and had to abandon the building project. He was the laughingstock of everyone who knew him because he had started something he couldn't finish.

Then Jesus tells the story about a king who started a war against a neighboring king without first calculating the military strength of his opponent. To his chagrin he soon realized that he had no hope of victory, so he was forced to try to negotiate a peace with his enemy.

The point of these two stories is simple—don't start if you aren't prepared to go all the way. Discipleship may cost you your life. If you aren't willing to pay the price of death on a cross, you cannot follow Jesus.

When Charles Lindberg made his first transatlantic flight, he was greeted in Europe by many reporters. One asked him, "Did you ever have any doubts that you would reach Europe?" He replied, "Do you think I'd have started if I thought I might make it only part way?" Don't ever start following Jesus with the idea that you can ditch the plane in mid-Atlantic. Don't even start following him with the thought that you can turn around at any point and return to your starting place. Don't start unless you are prepared to go all the way.

Thomas Paine wrote concerning the terrible conditions of Valley Forge during the winter of 1776. He said, concerning the revolutionary soldiers, "The summer soldier and the sunshine patriot will, in the crisis, shrink from the service of his country; but he that stands in it now deserves the love and thanks of man and woman." The "summer soldier" and the "sunshine patriot" refer to those who had joined the revolutionary army without realizing how cold the winter would be, how scarce the food would be, and how fierce the fighting would be. Thus, they would be tempted in the time of crisis, hardship, and privation to desert the cause of the Revolution.

Jesus is not interested in "summer soldiers" or "sunshine patriots." He is interested in those who are willing to give him their supreme loyalty and their absolute commitment.

They are willing not only to give up their families but also to give up their lives, if necessary, to follow him.

Unrestrained Sacrifice

The rival to Jesus does not have to be a person—either someone else or ourselves. It can be a business. It can be a home or a boat. It can be a hobby. It can be anything.

So the final demand of Jesus is total surrender. He says, "So therefore, no one of you can be My disciple who does not give up all his possessions" (v. 33, NASB). The words *give up* mean to "take leave of," "to renounce," or "to bid farewell to." Jesus demands that we not only be willing to give up our families and our lives but also our possessions. How better could he spell out total commitment than to say that he must come before our families, our lives, and our possessions?

Culbert Rutenber, the American Baptist preacher and teacher, declared that there are four kinds of conversion: doctrinal, emotional, moral, and total! Some people are converted to Christ doctrinally. They accept his teachings and begin to follow them. Others are converted emotionally. They are attracted by the person of Jesus and by his followers and are swept away by feelings of admiration. Others are converted morally. They recognize the high moral precepts of Jesus and seek to conform their lives to them. However, the kind of conversion that is necessary is a total conversion. It involves your mind, your heart, and your will—your whole life.

Salvation is total, and the Lord demands total discipleship. He does not save us in fractions, and he does not call us in fractions. He is not satisfied with one tenth of our money or one seventh of our time. He is interested not only in the tithe that we drop in the collection plate, but he is also interested in the other nine tenths. How we make it, how we manage it, how we feel toward it is as important as the portion we put in the collection plate. He is not only interested in how we use our time on Sunday, but he is also interested in the other six days. There can be no fractional discipleship. It is total surrender to Jesus Christ, or we cannot follow him.

A missionary returned to the United States after many years in China. As she gave her stirring testimony of all that Christ had done for her, the people were greatly moved. Afterwards a lady came to her and said, "I'd give the world to have your experiences." The missionary replied, "That's exactly what it cost me." We must be willing to give up the world if we are going to follow Jesus Christ.

Jesus closes out this teaching on the demands of discipleship with a strange saying. He said, "Salt is good; but if even salt has become tasteless, with what will it be seasoned? It is useless either for the soil or for the manure pile; it is thrown out" (vv. 34-35, NASB). What does this say to us? How does this fit in with what Jesus had just previously taught? Jesus is using salt as a symbol of discipleship. What is the distinctive quality of salt? It is not its color: many things are white. It is not its texture: there are many things that are granulated. The distinctive quality of salt is its taste: its tang. It is its saltiness. If salt loses that, it is worthless. You might as well throw it away.

Discipleship is like that. What is the distinctive quality of discipleship? It is sacrifice. Discipleship without sacrifice is like salt without flavor. It is useless and worthless. There is no need to try to follow Jesus unless you are willing to give him supreme loyalty, absolute commitment, and total surrender. Unless you are willing to put him before your family, your life, and your possessions, you cannot be his disciple.

When Billy Rose died, his rabbi said of him, "Whatever he was drawn to, it was always as if it were the single compulsion of his heart and mind. He never squeezed into a new door—he flung it wide open."

Jesus wants you to be his disciple. He invites you to come and follow him. But if you do so, understand the cost, and then do it with your whole heart. Don't try to squeeze in. Fling the door wide open, and follow him with all that is within you.

4. The Power of Personal, Persistent Prayer

Shortly before his drowning in 1956 Dawson Trotman, founder of the Navigators, interviewed one hundred missionary candidates for an evangelical mission board. He asked each one of them this question: "Do you have a systematic devotional life?"

A devotional life is a time when we meet God for prayer and Bible study on a daily basis. Only eight out of one hundred replied in the affirmative. A person might as well forget about following Christ and turn in his discipleship badge unless he or she is willing to pay the price of a disciplined devotional life.

Prayer is the breath of discipleship. It is as essential to our spiritual life as breathing is to our physical life. Ultimately, there is no personal religious life without prayer. We can have an institutional religious life without prayer but not a personal religious life. Unless we meet God in prayer, we do not meet him at all.

The measure of our immaturity and our pride is how long we think we can go without God and prayer. If you want to change your life, really change it, then I challenge you to develop a systematic devotional life.

Learn to meet God in prayer at the beginning of every day, and in six months you will be a different person. That's a money-back guarantee.

Jesus, God's Son, is our supreme example of the importance of prayer. If you will follow Jesus through any one of the four Gospels, marking the accounts that tell of his pray-

ing or his teachings about prayer, you will be amazed at the
place of prayer in his life. There are more commands in the
Bible to pray than there are to do anything else. And there
are more promises concerning prayer than anything else in
the Bible.

On one occasion, when Jesus had been praying, his disciples asked, "Lord, teach us to pray" (Luke 11:1). This is the
only thing that Jesus' disciples ever asked him to teach
them. They never asked him to teach them to preach. They
never asked that he teach them to perform miracles. They
never asked that he teach them to get along better with
other people. But they did ask him to teach them about
prayer. They obviously realized that this was the secret of
his great and wonderful life.

Jesus recognized that his disciples needed a recipe for
prayer, so he gave them one that we call the Lord's Prayer.
If you sent me into the kitchen to bake a cake, and you
didn't give me a recipe, I would end up making a mess.
After two or three messes, I would throw up my hands and
quit. That's the way people are with prayer. Without a
recipe they soon become discouraged and quit. So Jesus
gave us a recipe in the Lord's Prayer (Luke 11:1-4).

Did Jesus' disciples learn to pray? Look in on them in the
upper room after Jesus' ascension into heaven. They are not
trying to organize a Sunday School. They are not printing
bulletins. They are praying. As a result, the Holy Spirit
comes upon them on the day of Pentecost. Thereafter, there
are four things that they were continually devoting themselves to: the apostles' teachings, fellowship, the breaking
of bread, and prayer (Acts 2:42).

One of the greatest examples of the practice, priority, and
power of prayer in the New Testament church is found in
the story of Peter's deliverance from prison (Acts 12). King
Herod was doing evil to the church. He killed James, the

brother of John, with a sword. When he saw that this
pleased the religious leaders, he proceeded to arrest Peter
and put him in prison intending after the Passover to kill
him also.

This was a serious situation. The church appeared to be
helpless and hopeless in the face of Peter's arrest and approaching death. What could they do? They had no standing in the community. They had no friends in high places
who could pull political strings. They had no money. They
had no army to storm the jail and overcome the guards.
What could they do? Only one thing: they could pray. So
Luke records, "Prayer was made without ceasing of the
church unto God for him" (Acts 12:5).

Sometimes we find ourselves in this same situation. We
are sick, or some member of our family is critically ill. A
child is in trouble with the law. Our job is in jeopardy. We
feel absolutely helpless and hopeless. What can we do in
such an hour as that? We can still pray. We have not exhausted all of our resources until we have committed our
needs to God. No matter how dark the night, no matter
how hopeless the situation appears, no matter how difficult
the circumstances, we have never done all that we can do
until we have prayed.

When the church prayed, God performed a mighty mira-
cle. He sent his angel to the prison to rescue Peter. Peter
was asleep between two soldiers, bound with chains. The
angel tapped him on the side to awaken him. As he did the
chains fell from his hands, and the angel quickly led him to
safety out of the prison. At first Peter himself thought that
this was a dream. When he finally realized that he was
actually free he went to the house of Mary, the mother of
John Mark, where the church was gathered in prayer. He
knocked on the gate, and a young lady named Rhoda answered his knock. When she heard his voice she knew that
it was Peter. Without even opening the gate, she turned and

ran to tell the other disciples. But they didn't believe her.
Isn't that just like us? We pray for things but really don't
believe that they are going to happen. We ask God for
miracles, then we try to explain them away. It was only after
great insistence that Rhoda convinced them that Peter was
really standing outside the door. And when they saw him,
they were all astonished.

It was not many days after this that Herod, a proud and
pompous man, allowed the people to acclaim him as God.
Immediately the angels of the Lord struck him dead. With
Herod gone, the church enjoyed a period of peace and the
word of God multiplied.

A review of the events of this chapter bring several questions to mind. Why was James killed, and Peter delivered?
Couldn't God have saved James as well? Well, why didn't
he? The only answer that this chapter suggests is this:
"Prayer was made without ceasing of the church of God for
him" (Acts 12:5).

Prayer made the difference. The church prayed, and as
a result Peter was freed. Perhaps you are thinking, "If God
determined that James would die and Peter would be set
free, what difference did the prayer of the church make?"

First of all, prayer has the ability to postpone or delay
events—both the judgment of God or the victory of Satan
as in this case. James was killed, but Peter's execution was
postponed to a later date. Prayer may not remove the threat
entirely, but it can change the time schedule.

Second, prayer has the ability to give us peace in difficult
situations. There is a clear implication here that Peter was
at peace even though he was in prison. How could he sleep
on the night of his execution? If you knew that you were
going to be executed tomorrow morning—your head
would be chopped off—would you have a good night's
sleep tonight? Peter slept peacefully and soundly. It was not
that he was such a great man of faith—Peter was like us,

often weak and fearful—it was because the church was praying for him. That is why God gave him a peaceful heart. Prayer can do this for us also when we undergo times of difficulty and trouble.

Third, prayer can produce sudden changes like the removal of Herod. I don't think the church was praying for the king to die. We are not told in Scripture to pray in this way about those in authority. But the church was praying that God would intervene; as a result of their intercession God removed Herod altogether. This vicious, cruel tyrant to whom human life meant nothing was suddenly removed from the scene because the people who were responsive to God and depended upon him cried to him for his help.

What a marvelous challenge to prayer all of this is. Our God is a God of miracle-working power when his people pray. So we need to learn to pray big prayers.

John Newton wrote:

> Thou art coming to a King;
>   Large petitions with thee bring;
> For His grace and power are such,
>   None can ever ask too much.

But let me caution you. Make prayer your first choice, not your last resort. People say, "Pray for me; we've tried everything else." Is that a compliment to God? Let me ask you this: If you were God, wouldn't it be a compliment if the very first thing your children did was come to you for help? Nothing honors God more than to go to him the first thing. Make God your first choice and not your last chance.

Pray more from conviction and less from crisis. Most of our prayers are from crisis. We often don't pray until we have troubles or needs.

We ought to pray in advance. For example, we know that our children are going to get married one of these days. We ought to be praying for them and for their future marriages and prospective mates right now. If we prayed more from conviction, then we could pray less in crisis.

And we should not try to tell God what to do. We should just tell him our problems and let him do what he wants to do with them.

This experience teaches us three important lessons about when and how to pray. We should pray together, we should pray persistently, and we should pray specifically.

Harmony in Prayer

We know that we ought to pray privately. Jesus talked about entering into our closets to pray. We know also that we ought to pray together as families. But what about prayer in the church? Here is an encouragement to corporate prayer with the body of Christ. Luke tells us that prayer was made by "the church" unto God for Peter (Acts 12:5).

At the outset of his ministry Jesus said that his father's house should be called a house of prayer (Luke 19:46). When you think of God's house, do you think of it as a place of prayer? We usually think of it primarily as a place of preaching, a place of music, a place of teaching, and even a place of recreation. But few of us think of it as a place of prayer.

Jesus taught us to pray together. He said, "Again I say unto you, That if two of you shall agree on earth as touching any thing that they shall ask, it shall be done for them of my father which is in heaven" (Matt. 18:19). The Greek word translated "agree" in this verse is the root word from which we derive *symphony,* meaning literally "to be in accord" or "to sound together." There is tremendous power when the people of God harmonize together in prayer. The church ought to be offering up to God a great symphony of prayer continually.

To be sure, we ought to pray individually and privately. This is right and good. But we ought also to pray together.

A church requires togetherness. Halford Luccock said, "If a municipal water system is needed, it is not enough to encourage each citizen to dig his own well, but we must join together to create one great source of supply." Just so, the people of God need to pray together.

I'm Too Busy

Second, we need to pray persistently. The church in Jerusalem prayed "without ceasing." The words *without ceasing* literally mean "extended" or "outstretched." They prayed for an extended period of time. They stretched themselves out in prayer. They didn't pray just once or twice and quit. They prayed, and they kept on praying.

This is hard to do. It takes much discipline. It is hard to have a devotional life all the time. We already live full lives. So we think that we are too busy to pray. But did you read the newspaper this morning? Did you eat this morning? Do you watch television? Then you really do have time to pray. It is just a matter of priority.

The secret of discipleship is continuing to die to things that are good, so that we can live for the things that are better. You may have to die to the newspaper, so that you can live to the Bible.

Let me show you how you can find time to pray. What time do you get up in the morning? What time do you have breakfast? What time do you go to work? What time do you go to bed at night? These questions all indicate that we have some fixed points in our life. Starting at one of these fixed points we can set a time for prayer. Move back from your usual getting up time and get up thirty minutes earlier. Let that be your time alone with God. Unless we set such a regular time to pray, we will never pray like we ought to.

The secret to getting up early is to go to bed early. Someone has said, "You can't hoot with the owls at night and soar with the eagles during the day."

I like to pray in the morning for several reasons: one, the devil has been working all night, and if he is ever tired, he is tired in the mornings. Two, you almost always have God to yourself. Three, if you start the day right, it will more likely go right for you. As Henry Ward Beecher said, "The first hour of the morning is the rudder of the day."

But if it is difficult to begin a prayer life, it is even more difficult to continue one. One of the things that make it so difficult is that we easily become discouraged. If we do not receive the answer from God that we want, then we become discouraged and may quit our prayer time.

When we pray, we need to remember that there are at least four answers to prayer that God may give us. First, he may give us a direct answer. He sometimes answers exactly as we ask. Second, he may give us a denial. No is an answer just as much as yes is. Most of us have lived long enough to thank God that not all of our prayers have been answered. I have a friend who said, "If God had answered all of my prayers, I'd have as many wives as Brigham Young." If God had given me all that I asked for in the ignorance of childishness and selfishness, I would have destroyed myself. One of the signs that we are growing spiritually is that we get fewer and fewer no answers. We learn what not to ask for. The older our children get, the less often we ought to have to say no to them. That's partly because they have learned what not to ask for.

Third, God sometimes gives a different answer. He gives exceedingly abundantly above anything that we even think or ask. Saint Augustine tells in his *Confessions* how his pious mother, Monica, had begged God in prayer not to let her young son go to Italy and get away from her influence. But go to Italy Augustine did. What Monica did not know was that the bishop of Milan was the best equipped person in all the world to challenge the mind and the heart of her young, prodigious pagan.

Augustine went to hear Ambrose preach because of his reputation for rhetoric, but in the process what the bishop was saying as well as how he said it got through to Augustine. More than anyone else, Ambrose was used by God to reach this gifted young man.

Looking back on the whole thing, Augustine said, "God denied my mother the form of her request that he might eventually grant her the substance of her request."

And finally God sometimes gives us a delayed answer. People go astray waiting for an answer more than any other way. We have to learn to wait on God. In the example of Peter's deliverance, God waited until the very last night before he set his servant free. If the people had not persisted in prayer, they would have stopped too soon.

Call Me by Name

Third, we need to pray specifically. The Scriptures say that the church prayed without ceasing unto God "for him" (Acts 12:5). They prayed for Peter by name. They didn't pray, "God bless all the apostles," or "God bless all the people in jail." They prayed for Peter by name.

Some years ago, Josef Nordenhaug said to a group of Ridgecrest staffers, "Don't ever pray for me by simply saying, 'God bless all for whom we should pray.' That's typically American, the wholesale way, but please pray for me more personally."

That's exactly the way I feel. Pray retail and not wholesale for me. Wholesale is praying like this, "Lord, bless me and all my folks. Forgive me of all of my sins, and guide me today. And PS, Lord, bless all the missionaries around the world." We can pray that way, and in fifteen seconds a day we can cover everything and everybody in the whole world. We need to pray specifically, and we should thank God specifically for things. We ought to call people by name. And we should ask for forgiveness of specific sins.

We don't sin wholesale, do we? If we sinned wholesale, I think that God would give us permission to repent wholesale. But we don't. Learn to pray specifically, and you will likely receive more specific answers to your prayers.

Finally, we should pray in Jesus' name. Jesus said, "Whatsoever you ask in My name, that will I do, that the Father may be glorified in the Son" (John 14:13, NASB). In this verse Jesus gives us the privilege of using his name in prayer.

On our own we are not worthy to approach the Holy throne of God. But through Jesus our advocate, we have free access to God in prayer. The Bible says, "Seeing then that we have a great high priest, that is passed into the heavens, Jesus the Son of God, . . . Let us therefore come boldly unto the throne of grace" (Heb. 4:14-16).

God, for Christ's sake, forgives our sin. God, for Christ's sake, supplies our needs. God, for Christ's sake, receives our prayers. And the person who comes with confidence to the throne of grace sees that this approach to God has been made possible because of Jesus Christ.

Many may ask, "Is there no other way to pray except through Jesus Christ?" You may try, but according to the Bible, "There is one God, and one mediator between God and men, the man Christ Jesus" (1 Tim. 2:5).

A disciple is a person who not only accepts Jesus as Lord and Savior, but he or she also recognizes him as high priest and daily approaches God in prayer through Jesus. That is a part of what it means to be a disciple.

5. Feasting on the Word of God

People often come to me saying that they want to be better Christians. When they do I remind them that there is no magical switch that they can flick that will suddenly make them more Christlike. Becoming a good Christian is like becoming a good husband or wife. You start from a point of commitment, and you grow into it. We can become a Christian in an instant, but there is no instant maturity. If we have the desire, the discipline, and the determination, then in time we can grow to be a good disciple.

One thing that is necessary to becoming a better Christian is to study the Word of God on a regular basis. The Scriptures are our spiritual food. The apostle Peter compared them to a baby's milk (1 Pet. 2:1-2). Just as a newborn baby needs and desires milk to grow physically, so we need and should desire the Word of God that we may grow to spiritual maturity.

If we are going to be a disciple, we must from the first get a grip on the milk bottle and keep feeding on God's Word. I use the word *grip* because one of Satan's tactics is to snatch the Word of God away from us to keep us from growing as we should. In the parable of the sower, Jesus told of a man who went forth to sow. Some of the seeds fell on hard ground, and the birds came and plucked them away, and they bore no fruit. Later as he interpreted this parable he identified the seed as the Word of God, the hard soil as men's hearts, and the birds as Satan who desires to snatch God's Word away from us before it can bear fruit

(Matt. 13:1-19). So according to Jesus, one of Satan's desires is to rip the Word of God out of our hearts. If, then, we are going to grow as disciples, we must have a good grip on God's Word to keep him from doing that.

There are five ways for us to get a firm grip on the Bible. We need to hear, to read, to study, to meditate upon, and to live God's Word. Doing all five of these things will help us to get a strong grip on the Word of God. Omit any one of them, and you weaken your grip on the Scriptures.

Let me illustrate what I am talking about by using the five fingers on your hand to represent these five ways to grasp God's Word. The little finger represents hearing the Word of God. If you try to pick up your Bible with just your little finger alone, you will find it impossible. Just so, you can hear the finest preachers and teachers in the world and never get a grasp of the Bible as you should by that alone.

Next, let your thumb represent reading the Word of God. If you use your little finger and your thumb you will be able to pick the Bible up and get a slight grip on it. However, your grip will be weak, and the Book can easily be snatched from you.

Then let your ring finger represent studying the Word of God. Add it to your grip, and you have a stronger hold on the Scriptures.

Next let your middle finger represent meditation. When it is added to your grip, it becomes stronger still. Finally, let your index finger represent application of the Word of God to your life. When it is added, your fingers all together form a vicelike grip making it difficult to jerk the Bible out of your hand. Just so, if you hear, read, study, meditate, and live God's Word, Satan will find it difficult to snatch the Bible out of your heart. Eliminate any one of these practices, and you lessen your hold on the Word of God.

I have an uncle who was involved in an accident years ago; his index finger and his middle finger were cut off.

Through the years he has had a very difficult time doing normal things like tying a shoe lace or buttoning a shirt. It most certainly has affected his ability to grip things. In the same way if you eliminate any one of these practices from your life, your grip on God's Word will be lessened.

If you want to be a better Christian, then you need to practice all five of these things. There are admonitions to do all of them in Paul's two letters to Timothy. Let's look at these five practices as set out by Paul and see how they can help us to be better disciples.

He That Hath Ears to Hear

The first thing we must do if we want a good grasp of the Bible is to hear the Word of God (2 Tim. 1:13; 2:2). God has given to his church gifted teachers and preachers to help bring us to Christian maturity. It is therefore our responsibility to put ourselves under the ministry of these people, so that we can grow and become all that God desires of us. That is why Jesus kept saying, "He that hath ears to hear, let him hear" (Matt. 11:15).

To hear the Word of God is the first responsibility of every Christian. There are times when a preacher does not feel like preaching and does not feel particularly inspired, but he must deliver a message anyhow. And there are times when we don't feel like listening to a message, but we have the responsibility of listening anyway. Even when we don't feel like listening God speaks to us, and we are blessed in our hearing.

One way for you to increase your hearing ability is to begin taking notes on the sermons that you hear. When sermons go in one ear and out the other, you only remember about 15 percent of what you hear. However, when a sermon goes in your ear, runs down the muscle structure of your arm, then flows out of the end of your fingers, and through the point of a pen onto a piece of paper, it etches itself in your mind. You actually increase your hearing ability by 300 percent when you take notes.

How do you take notes on a sermon? Write down the subject, the text, the main points of the sermon, and then ideas that are especially striking to you. It is better that you leave church with one or two sentences from God than to leave and have no recollection of what was said at all. Most people leave church with no message at all.

Taking notes in church can also provide material for family devotion throughout the week. If several members of the family are taking notes, then you can share what impressed you most about the message during your family devotional time and thus get a double blessing from each message.

Readers Are Leaders

The second thing that will help you to get a grip on the Bible is to read it. Paul told Timothy to give attention to reading until he came again (1 Tim. 4:13). If any sincere seeker will keep an open mind, prayerfully and slowly read the Bible for a year especially the Gospels, it is practically certain that something important will occur in his life. If he stays close enough to the central fire for a sufficient period, he is likely to be ignited.

The Bible unfortunately is the least read best-seller in all of history. If all the neglected Bibles were dusted simultaneously, we would have a record dust storm, and the sun would go into eclipse for a whole week.

Mark Twain once humorously commented about his father. "When I was fourteen," he reminisced, "I felt that my father was so dumb that it was embarrassing to have him around. When I was twenty-one, I was amazed at what he'd learned in just seven years." Some people haven't read the Bible in so long that they would be absolutely amazed at the wisdom found in it. If they would just take time to read it, they would be enriched by it.

How do we read the Bible? Martin Luther said that he studied the Bible as one would gather apples: "First, I shake the whole tree, that the ripest might fall. Then I climb the tree and shake each limb, and then each branch, and then each twig, and then I look under each leaf."

We need to approach the Word of God with the same kind of diligence. We need to read the Bible prayerfully, carefully, systematically, and trustfully. Read a book of the Bible through in one sitting. Read the same book again and again. Slowly read the Bible in many different translations, and ask God to teach you what is in it. Take a notebook and write notes as you read, then you'll get excited and start telling others about it.

The average man could read the Bible through in just a year while waiting for his wife to get ready to go out. The average woman could read the Bible through in a year just waiting for her husband to get to the supper table after she has called him. So whatever you do, and however you do it, make sure you get into a regular study of God's Word.

Knowing and Growing Christians

The third thing that will give you a grip on the Bible is to study it. Paul wrote to Timothy, "Study to shew thyself approved unto God, a workman that needeth not to be ashamed, rightly dividing the word of truth" (2 Tim. 2:15). The difference in reading the Bible and studying the Bible is the difference between waterskiing and scuba diving. When you water-ski you just skim across the top of the water and enjoy the beauty of what you can see as you skip by. When you scuba dive, you go down deep into the water and see things that you never dreamed were there. Reading the Word of God can be enjoyable, but studying the Word of God can be more profitable. In fact, if you will go down deep into it you will discover a beauty and a treasure that will bless your life forever.

Peter encourages us to "grow in grace, and in the knowledge of our Lord and Saviour Jesus Christ" (2 Pet. 3:18). Studying the Bible is essential for this kind of growing. If you want to be a knowing and growing Christian, then you must hear, read, and study the Word of God.

Take a Second Look

The fourth way to get a grip on Scripture is to meditate upon it. Paul commanded Timothy, "Meditate upon these things; give thyself wholly to them; that thy profiting may appear to all" (1 Tim. 4:15). The word *profiting* literally means advancement, progress, or growth. It is through meditation that we advance, progress, and grow the most in our Christian lives. The Greek word for meditation literally means "to attend." It suggests that we are to hear, read, and study God's Word with both attention and intention. Meditation is the doorway to application; it is never an end in itself. Meditation is not just for gratification but for application and edification.

Meditation allows you to apply the Word of God to your heart and life. The Hebrew word for meditate describes a cow who chews her cud. A cow chews her cud up, down, and around, swallows it, and then brings it back up and chews on it some more. It goes down into her stomach, pops back up into her mouth, and she chews it again. So the word *meditate* means that you let what you have already learned come back into your mind so that it can be reviewed and pondered. Meditation is reflective thinking with a view to application.

Meditating and memorizing the Word of God will give you strength and guidance in the hour of temptation and wisdom in the hour of opportunity. At the outset of his ministry, Jesus went into the wilderness where he fasted forty days. During that time Satan came tempting him to go contrary to the will of God. Jesus met each temptation with a scriptural quotation. As Satan enticed him to do wrong Jesus replied by saying, "It is written" (Matt. 4:4-10). Jesus had both guidance and strength in the hour of testing because as a child he had meditated upon and memorized the Word of God. When the hour of stress and enticement came, he was sustained through Scripture.

Jesus had to have God's Word stored in his heart because he had no Bible of his own to carry around. In Jesus' day Scriptures were copied by hand on huge scrolls. They were so large and so expensive that no one had a copy of his own. It was not until the 1400s and the invention of the printing press and loose-leaf binding that the average person could own a copy of the Scriptures. Since that time, we have been able to reduce printing and binding of the Bible into smaller and smaller sizes. I have in my possession a copy of the smallest Bible in the world. It is a reproduction of a 1,245 page edition of the Bible—both the Old and New Testaments—reduced to a one-and-one-half-inch square, plastic slide. It contains every verse, chapter, book, and each of the 773,746 words of the Bible. And it can be read with an ordinary student's microscope of 100x or more.

But Jesus had no such Bible. In fact, he didn't even have a pocket New Testament. The only Scriptures he had were those that he had stored up in his heart as a child. But in the hour of temptation, those Scriptures sustained him for victorious living.

When the apostles gave witness to Christ in their world, they did so by quoting Old Testament Scriptures which they had memorized. Stephen's defense of the faith is an example of how the early Christians used Scripture which they had meditated upon and memorized (Acts 7). From these examples it follows that meditation and memorization will help us in both our days of temptation and our hours of opportunity.

Growing Up or Growing Older

The fifth thing we need to do to get a grip on the Bible is to live God's Word. Paul admonished Timothy to "continue" in the things which he had learned (2 Tim. 3:14). It is not enough just to hear, read, study, or meditate upon God's Word. If we want to really have it in our lives, it must be lived on a daily basis.

James, the brother of our Lord, warned us not to be hearers of the Word only but to be doers as well. That's the only way we retain and profit from Scripture (Jas. 1:22-25).

There are many people cruising from church to church, from Bible conference to Bible conference, filling notebook after notebook, wearing out Bible after Bible, who are still some of the crankiest, fussiest, most irresponsible people you meet. Why? Because they do not practice what they hear. A person would be foolish to go to his physician for a diagnosis of an ailment and then think that just because he had talked with his doctor he would suddenly get well. No, he would have to take the medicine, have the surgery, or whatever is prescribed by the doctor if he wants to get well. Likewise, just being exposed to the truth won't make us mature. No matter how reliable the teaching, or how gifted the teacher, the declaration of truth alone does not provide the removal of difficulties.

Think of the Scriptures as an absolutely accurate map that tells you how to get to a certain destination. But just looking at a map won't automatically transport you to your desired destination. Getting to that place means that you have to make the effort, pay the cost, take the time for travel, and stay at it until you arrive.

So it is in the Christian life. God's map is reliable and available. It is also clear and direct. But there is no hocus-pocus in its pages that automatically sends its readers by way of magic carpet to maturity.

A disciple is one who is involved in practicing on a regular, consistent basis what he or she hears and takes in. You see, it is one thing to grow old in the Lord, but it is another thing to grow up in the Lord.

Remember that I said at the beginning of this chapter that you only remember about 15 percent of what you hear. However, when you live the Word of God, it becomes an inseparable part of you.

Remember also that we are in a spiritual struggle, and one of Satan's primary desires is to snatch the Word of God from our hearts. Until we apply these five practices to the Bible, we will not be able to retain its message or to be the disciples we ought to be.

One of the ways to get the most out of the Bible or any book is to find out why the author wrote it. You would not read the phone book to learn how to raise a garden. You would not read the dictionary to find an airline's flight schedule. You would not read a cookbook to know how to service your car. Obviously, that is not the reason why those books were written. To get the most out of the Bible, you need to know why it was written. It was given to introduce us to Jesus Christ who is both Lord and Savior. Once we know him as Lord and Savior and through faith in him are born into the kingdom of God, the Bible can become spiritual food to help us to grow in our discipleship.

6. Understanding the Word of God

Leroy (Satchel) Paige was the first black pitcher in the American League. He broke into the majors as a rookie at forty-two years of age. After his first pitching exhibition, he was asked by his new manager, "Do you throw that hard consistently?" "No, sir," said Satchel, "I do it all the time."

Consistency is one of the marks of a disciple. Jesus said that we are his disciples if we "continue" in his word (John 8:31). And the apostle Paul in discipling Timothy encouraged him to "continue" in the Scriptures which had brought him to salvation through faith in Christ (2 Tim. 3:14-15). So a disciple is one who continues consistently in God's Word.

Paul told Timothy two things about the Scriptures that we all need to know. He told him how they came, and why they came. First, they came by inspiration of God. The word *inspired* means "God breathed." Peter tells us that the Holy Scriptures are a result of holy men being "moved" by the Holy Ghost (2 Pet. 1:21). The word *moved* literally means "to be borne along" or "to be driven." It describes a ship whose sails have been filled with wind and is driven forward by the power of that wind. Just so, the Holy Spirit of God moved upon holy men, drove them, and pushed them to write the Holy Scriptures.

Paul is specific. "All" Scripture is inspired. That means that every part of it is inspired. A businessman inexperienced in presiding at church meetings followed up the Scripture reading with: "If there are no *corrections* or *addi-*

63

tions, the Scriptures will stand approved as read." The Scriptures do not need any additions or corrections, and their reliability does not depend upon our approval. They are all inspired, and thus they are truth without any mixture of error.

In a society that changes as rapidly as ours does, big question marks are raised about absolutes. What can I believe? To what should I be committed? What is there in life that is lasting and permanent? We once assumed, for example, that air was always safe to breathe, that water was always safe to drink, that policemen were always honest, that doctors always came when they were called, that policemen could always be trusted, that newspapers always told the truth, that preachers always believed what they preached, that right was always right, and wrong was always wrong. But changes have shaken all of these assumptions. What can a person believe in today's world? We can still anchor our lives to the Word of God. It is completely reliable and trustworthy in matters of faith and practice.

The purpose of God's Word's coming to us is that we might be "perfect" and completely equipped for every good work. The word *perfect* is that Greek word *teleios* that I explained in chapter 2. Remember that the word does not mean sinless perfection. It means "mature," "whole," or "complete." The purpose of the Bible is to bring us to mature, spiritual personhood.

But one of the major problems we face is how to interpret the Bible. There are more than 222 different denominations in America, and almost every one of them claims the Bible as their final authority. Which one is right? Understanding the Bible and interpreting the Bible correctly is essential for the modern-day disciple.

There are five principles that will help us in interpreting the Bible. They are the linguistic principle, the historical principle, the theological principle, the practical principle, and the spiritual principle. If you will use these five principles in studying and interpreting the Bible, you will better understand the Word of God that you are to continue in.

The Word and Words

The first principle of biblical interpretation we should use is the linguistic principle. The Word of God has come to us in words. If we are to know and understand God's Word, we must understand the meaning of the words through which it has come. The problem is that the Word was first delivered to us in the Hebrew, Greek, and Aramaic languages.

This is good news and bad news. The good news is that the Greek language in which the New Testament was written is one of the most precise and expressive languages ever known. English, on the other hand, is a strange language. In our language "a fat chance" and "a slim chance" mean the same thing. But, on the other hand, "a wise guy" and "a wise man" are altogether different. So God chose to speak to us in a language that is much more precise and expressive than our own.

The bad news is that most people cannot read the Greek language. Since this is true, there are two things that can help us to know the exact meaning of the words that God used to speak to us. The first is a modern translation of the Bible, and the second is a concordance.

The most popular version of the Bible to most people is the King James Version translated from the Hebrew and the Greek into the English language in 1611 AD. The difficulty with this version of the Bible is that words, like children, never stand still; they are always growing and developing and changing. In fact, there is about a 17 percent language drift in word meaning every one-hundred years. Since the King James Version was translated into the

English over 370 years ago, much of its language is now out of date.

Let me illustrate. Back in 1675, some nine years after the terrible London fire, Sir Christopher Wren himself laid the first foundation stone in what was to be his greatest enterprise: the building of Saint Paul's Cathedral. It took him thirty-five long years to complete this task, and when it was done he waited breathlessly for the reaction of Her Majesty, Queen Anne. After being carefully shown through the structure, she summed up her feelings for the architecture in three words: "It is awful; it is amusing; it is artificial." Imagine how you would feel if words like these were used to describe the work of your life. However, Sir Christopher Wren's biographer said that on hearing these words he heaved a sigh of relief and bowed gratefully before his sovereign. How could this be? The explanation is simple: in 1710 the word *awful* meant "awe inspiring." The word *amusing* meant "amazing," and the word *artificial* meant "artistic." What to our ears sounds like devastating criticism was at that time words of measured praise.

This sort of thing happens all the time, for words have a life of their own and are forever undergoing a change in meaning. We can readily see that happening about us today. For example, there was a time when "grass" was something we mowed. Today it might mean something a person smokes. There was a time when "fuzz" was something that grew on a peach. Today it might mean a policeman. There was a time when "bread" was something we baked in an oven. Today it might mean money. There was a time when "turkey" was something we ate at Thanksgiving. Today it might be a term of derision.

Since words are always changing, it is necessary to produce new translations of the Bible continually so that we have God's original Word in words we can understand today.

Another help in understanding the original words of the Bible is a concordance. A concordance is an alphabetical index of all the major words of the Bible. It will tell you the meaning of those words in the Greek and the Hebrew and where those words are found in the Bible. The concordance is the second most important book to the Bible if you want to study the Bible seriously.

Let me show you how a concordance works. Look for a moment at the verse, "Casting all your care upon him; for he careth for you" (1 Pet. 5:7). There are three key words in this verse. They are the word *care,* the word *casting,* and the word *careth.* Now look up each of those words in the concordance, and you will see their exact meaning. The word *care* means "distractions, anxieties, or worries." It is the same word that was used by Jesus when he said, "Take no thought for your life, what ye shall eat, or what ye shall drink; nor yet for your body, what ye shall put on" (Matt. 6:25).

Next, look at the word *casting.* It means "to lay upon." It is the same word that is used to describe the disciples throwing their clothing as a saddle blanket on the colt Jesus used for his triumphal entry into the city of Jerusalem. Then look at the word *careth.* It means "to be of interest" or "to be concerned" or "it matters."

Put these all together, and you get the full impact of Peter's admonition. He is urging us to put all of our worries and cares upon the Lord in the same way that a person would put a saddle blanket on a horse; because we are of interest to him, he is concerned about us; we matter to him. Understanding these words literally makes the Word of God come alive to us.

Making a Sandwich

The second principle of Bible interpretation that we should use is the historical principle. This includes a study of the author, time, place, circumstances, and context of the writing. Involved in the historical principle are studies of biblical geography, biblical history, biblical culture, and related subjects.

The context of a verse or a passage is of utmost importance. In ordinary life we understand the importance of context. For a farmer, a donkey means a beast of burden. In the context of a national election in the United States, it means the Democratic party. The word *Yankee* is different in Civil War context than in a baseball context. And so, we should seek to find the particular context of the biblical verse and as much other historical data as we can.

Look at 1 Peter 5:7 as the meat of this passage. The verses on either side are slices of bread. The whole flavor of the passage is to be found in all of them together. The fact that these words come from the pen of Peter the apostle also gives them more meaning. They are an encouragement to humility and to trust in the Lord and not in ourselves because Satan is always close at hand.

No doubt these words came out of Peter's own experience of failure. The Lord had warned him of Satan's desire to "sift" him (Luke 22:31), but he was too proud and self-sufficient to admit his need. The end result was that he on one occasion denied the Lord three times. But to his utter amazement the Lord did not cease to care for him. He rather came to him and reinstated him to his apostleship.

Out of this bitter experience Peter warns us to humble ourselves before the Lord and to trust ourselves to him completely, so Satan will not have an advantage over us. Peter teaches us that there is an absolute relationship between casting our cares upon the Lord and not being overcome by Satan.

Another example might help. The historical background of 1 Corinthians 11:5 reveals that the wearing of a veil was a means of indicating a chaste woman in the Corinth of

Paul's day. In this context we understand why the apostle admonished Christian women to keep their heads covered. In days when the infant Christian movement could be misunderstood, he did not want the women of the church to be mistaken for religious prostitutes. Short hair and the lack of a veil would have put a woman under suspicion. So an understanding of the historical facts concerning the passage is important in making a correct interpretation of it.

The Object and the End of the Scripture

A third principle of biblical interpretation that we should use is the theological principle. The Bible is to be understood from its center, its heart, its Christ. This principle includes doctrinal interpretation. Included is the idea that difficult verses or verses on the periphery must be understood in the light of the plainest passages.

Christ is the center of biblical truth, the object and end of all scriptural revelation. He is the central figure of the whole Book, and directly or indirectly every passage in the Word points to Jesus. Until we have caught a glimpse of him in a passage we have studied, we have not yet gotten to the bottom of it.

Jesus said, "Search the scriptures; for in them ye think ye have eternal life: and they are they which testify of me" (John 5:39). On one occasion Jesus began "at Moses and all the prophets" and "expounded unto them in all the scriptures the things concerning himself" (Luke 24:27).

That must have been a wonderful experience, don't you think? Can you imagine how those disciples must have felt as Jesus shared with them the Scriptures which showed them pictures of himself. All the Bible points to the Lord Jesus, so in a real sense of the word we can say the Bible is a "Him" book. Jesus is its central figure. Jesus is the main personality. All of the pathways of the Scriptures ultimately lead to the Son of God. The Bible is like a vast art gallery in which there are many different pictures of the same personality.

I heard about a little chapel in the Italian Alps which had an unusual arrangement of statues in it. In the center of the chapel is a statue of Christ. Down the inner walls of the chapel are statues of the Old Testament prophets all pointing toward the focal point of the little chapel, Jesus Christ. Whoever designed that chapel and those statues understood the foundational truth that all the Old Testament points to Jesus Christ. More than that, all the Gospels center around Christ. And all the Epistles look back to Christ.

An old preacher once said to a young one, "My son, Christ is the key that unlocks every Scripture. If you have any trouble finding the meaning of a certain passage, try putting Christ right in the middle and see how it will brighten up." You try that for yourself, and you, too, will see that this rule works from the beginning of the Bible to the end.

Now, go back to the passage concerning the cares of life. The theological principle of this passage is that God loves us so much that he gave his very Son to die for us. So we need to put our worries in his hands. When all of our worries are in God's hands, Satan cannot get to us.

Don't Be a Yo-Yo Christian

The fourth principle of biblical interpretation that we should use is called the practical principle. This principle places emphasis on the edifying aspects of the Bible for today.

The Bible must not be read simply to gain information. It must be read to change our lives. The writer of Hebrews said, "Without faith it is impossible to please him" (Heb. 11:6). We should respond in faith to what we read in the Bible and begin to practice it. This is exactly where Israel failed. "The word preached did not profit them, not being mixed with faith in them that heard it" (Heb. 4:2).

Paul Little, in his book *How to Give Away Your Faith,* suggests several direct questions we should ask about any passage we are studying: "Is there an example to follow? Is there a sin to be avoided? Is there a command to be obeyed? Is there a promise to be claimed? What does this particular passage teach me about God or about Jesus Christ? Is there a difficulty here to be explored? Is there anything in this passage that I should pray about today?"

So, try to relate every passage you study to some personal need in your life. The passage in 1 Peter 5:7 says that God loves us, so we should let him do our worrying for us. We should not be a "yo-yo Christian" who keeps laying his cares upon the Lord and then snatching them back again.

The Secret Things of God

The fifth principle of biblical interpretation that we should use is the spiritual principle. At the beginning of every Bible study we should pray and ask God to guide us. Why? Because the Holy Spirit who inspired the Scriptures is able to enlighten our minds with regard to the meaning of them. Thus, the psalmist prayed, "Open thou mine eyes, that I may behold wondrous things out of thy law" (Ps. 119:18). Prayer like that is a reminder that the human intellect unaided cannot grasp the true significance of Scripture.

If you have difficulty understanding the meaning of certain verses, then give the Lord credit for knowing more than you understand. Remember that the secret things belong to the Lord.

So when you pray over the passage in 1 Peter 5:7, remember to thank the Lord that he cares about all of your cares, and ask him to help you not to worry but to trust him more.

We never meet in person most of the authors of the books we read. We know very little about them. However,

their writings accomplish the main purpose. We absorb the
message or we are inspired by the thoughts or we are enter-
tained by their story. We can understand the average book
without knowing the author.

But the Bible is different. Until we know the Author of
the Bible, we cannot know the Book itself. If we want to
understand the Bible, we must be acquainted with the di-
vine Author of the Bible. We need that personal knowledge
of God that comes when we trust Jesus as our Savior. When
this happens, we are given the spiritual eyesight that is
essential to study the Bible. James Hamilton was right: "A
Christian on his knees sees farther than a philosopher on his
tiptoes."

It takes the eyes of an artist to appreciate great art and the
ears of a musician to understand fine music, and it takes the
eyes and ears and heart of the soul opened by the spirit of
God to understand the wonders of God's Word.

Like "Satchel" Paige's pitching exhibition, we need not
only to study the Bible consistently, but we also need to do
it all the time. That's a part of what it means to be a disciple.

7. Think Globally, Act Locally

Shortly after I became a Christian as a teenage boy, my home church had a special week of study of the book *Every Christian's Job* by C. E. Matthews. The thesis of the study was that every Christian should be a witness for Jesus Christ. Being a new Christian, I believed that I should do everything that Jesus told me to do. Since I had not grown up in a Christian home, and since I had had no opportunity to observe Christians in the church I didn't know any better than to believe that. Whatever Jesus said do, I thought I was supposed to do. So I started trying to share my faith at home, with my classmates at school, and on the job.

It was years later as I began to study the Bible on my own that I came to realize just how central witnessing is to the Christian faith, and how crucial it is to discipleship. Witnessing, evangelism, and missions were at the heart of Jesus' ministry. He came to seek and to save those who were lost. And he busied himself about this work continually. When he met the woman at the well he did not discuss with her water pollution, but he told her about living water, and she was saved. When he talked with Nicodemus, a ruler of the Jews, he did not discuss the political situation of Palestine. He rather told Nicodemus how to be born again. When he counseled with the rich young ruler, he didn't talk to him about economics. He told him how he could find true riches in heaven. And when he went home with Zacchaeus, the tax collector, he did not discuss tax reforms; he brought salvation to his house. Jesus was ever and always an evangelist, a missionary, and a bringer of good news.

As he called his twelve apostles, he trained, organized, and sent them out to evangelize also. Later in his ministry, he enlisted seventy others whom he sent out in the same way (Luke 10:1). And before his crucifixion he said, "As my Father hath sent me, even so send I you" (John 20:21).

After his resurrection and before his ascension, Jesus said, "All power is given unto me in heaven and in earth. Go ye therefore, and teach all nations, baptizing them in the name of the Father, and of the Son, and of the Holy Ghost: Teaching them to observe all things whatsoever I have commanded you: and, lo, I am with you alway, even unto the end of the world" (Matt. 28:18-20). These words have been called the Great Commission. They are in fact the commission of every disciple. They set out for us the work of every individual believer as well as every church. We are to make disciples by witnessing, mark them by baptism, and mature them by teaching them all the things that Jesus commanded us.

Some Christians seem to feel no responsibility for this kind of going and witnessing. They say, "People know where the church is; if they want to come to it they can do it." However, knowing where you ought to be doesn't mean you know how to get there. A boy scout lost in the woods may know very well where he ought to be—back at the camp. However, the fact that he is lost means he doesn't know how to get there. He needs someone to guide him. People who are spiritually lost need guidance also. Jesus never suggested that worldlings should come to the church. But he did command the church to go into the world to witness. Since Jesus is our example as well as our Savior, we need to go after the lost as he did.

Some Christians feel that they have no right to witness. They say, "A person's relationship to God is a private affair.

It is none of my business. I have no right to interfere." If you feel that way, you don't understand God's command and Christ's authority. If the police thought I was dealing in marijuana, do you think they would hesitate to interrogate me? If the IRS thought I was not paying my taxes, do you think they would hesitate to audit me? If I owned a restaurant, and the county health officials felt that I was not keeping it clean, do you think they would hesitate closing me down? By what authority do the police question my actions? By what authority does the IRS question my tax paying? By what authority does the health office question my cleanliness? They have authority vested in them by the government.

By the same token, I am a person under authority. Jesus told me to go, and I must do it or be guilty of insubordination. Making disciples through evangelism and missions is my main business.

Nothing we do is quite as important as winning people to Jesus Christ. Dr. L. Nelson Bell, the father-in-law of Billy Graham, gave twenty-five years of his life to serving the people of China as a missionary-surgeon. He helped build and operate a large missionary hospital. It was recognized around the world. They had a full-time Bible evangelist who witnessed to every patient. Later in his life when he was moderator of the Presbyterian Church in the United States, someone asked him how many of his former patients were still living. He replied that most likely 98 percent of them would be dead by now. Then he added, "Which shows that what we did for them spiritually is what really matters."

It is important that the hungry be fed. It is important that the naked be clothed. It is important that the poor be housed. It is important that the sick be healed. It is important that the illiterate be taught. But it is imperative that the

lost be saved. What is a man profited if he shall gain the
whole world and lose his own soul?

Any Christian who does not recognize the need for and
the responsibility to be a witness, a missionary, and an
evangelist has not the slightest idea of what discipleship is
all about. The prayer then of every one of us ought to be:

> God help me see in all I meet,
> In country road or city street,
> Not just people passing by,
> But poor lost souls for whom Christ did die.

Not only does the ministry of Jesus, the example of Jesus,
and the commission of Jesus indicate that we are to be busy
about witnessing, but the figures and symbols used for disciples in the Bible spotlight this also. There are three of them
that are especially impressive: fishermen, laborers, and ambassadors.

First, Jesus compared us to fishermen. He said, "Follow
me, and I will make you fishers of men" (Matt. 4:19). To
most of us today, fishing is just a sport. It is something we
do in our pastime for fun. However, Jesus was talking to
professionals when he said those words. Fishing was a matter of life and death to them. To those men who fished for
a living, Jesus said, "Up until now you have caught fish for
men. From henceforth you shall catch men for God." Those
very words to those men indicate that witnessing and soul-
winning can never be a casual, part-time activity to us. We
are to give ourselves wholeheartedly to reaching others for
Christ.

The second symbol that Jesus used for his disciples' work
was that of a laborer. He said, "The harvest truly is plente-
ous, but the labourers are few; Pray ye therefore the Lord
of harvest, that he will send forth labourers into his harvest"
(Matt. 9:37-38). All of us know that there are seasons when
a farmer's life is reasonably relaxed. But that is not true of

the harvest season. When the crop is ripe in the field, there is an urgency to get it in.

My first two pastorates were in farming communities. When the crops were ready for harvest, the farmers worked from sunup to sundown seven days a week. They sometimes put headlights on their tractors and combines and worked late into the night. Their fields of grain represented a sizable financial investment and months of labor and toil. It was of great value to them. Every day they delayed increased the risk of losing the crop. So they went about their work with urgency and diligence. So Jesus used this terminology to impress upon us the urgency of witnessing.

My favorite analogy for our task as disciples is that of an ambassador. Paul declares that we are ambassadors for Christ. We are to speak in his place. We urge the world to become reconciled to God through him (2 Cor. 5:20). An ambassador is a legate of the emperor or the king. He serves in a foreign land, represents his own kingdom, and knows that his kingdom is judged by himself. What he is, what he does, and what he says all reflect upon his native land. His voice is the voice of his king.

I have made several trips to Belize, Central America. The Baptist manse we stayed in on two of our trips is located next to the American consulate. The last time I was there I noticed a sign at the driveway of the consulate building that said, "Do not even think of parking here." We have all seen signs that say, "No parking," or "Please do not block the driveway." But this one said, "Do not even think of parking here." When I read that sign, my first thought was, *What a turkey that consul must be!* It is no wonder that America has such a bad image around the world. To a measure, all US citizens are judged by that one man because he is our official representative to that foreign country.

We are ambassadors for Christ. He is our King, heaven is our home, and we are here on this earth as his representa-

tives. We speak in his place. We represent his cause. We
urge all men everywhere to be reconciled to God through
him.

As ambassadors for Christ we represent him, we witness
for him by what we are, what we do, and what we say. Our
attitudes, our actions, as well as our appeals bear witness for
Christ.

There are always those who try to set living the gospel
and sharing the gospel over against one another. I like what
Paul E. Little said in his book *How To Give Away Your Faith.*
"Which is more important in witnessing, the life I live or
the words I say? This question throws the consistency of our
lives and our verbal witness into a false antithesis. It's like
asking which wing of an airplane is more important, the
right or the left! Obviously, both are essential, and you
don't have anything without both. Life and lip are inseparable in effective witnessing for Christ." So, by what we are,
what we do, what we say, we are to bear witness to Christ.

Think Globally, Act Locally

First, we represent Christ by what we are. Before His
ascension Jesus said, "But ye shall receive power after that
the Holy Ghost is come upon you: and you shall be witnesses unto me both in Jerusalem and in Judea, and in
Samaria, and unto the uttermost parts of the earth" (Acts
1:8).

Jesus did not say to us, "Do witnessing." He said, "Be
witnesses." How easily we fall into the trap of doing witnessing and not being witnesses. Witnessing and evangelism always begin with "being." They depend on what we
are.

Jesus also told us to begin where we are and to keep
working until we have preached unto the ends of the earth.
That means that we are to think globally but act locally.
Where does our world begin? It begins at the tip of our toes

and extends to the uttermost part of the globe. So we are to begin by winning people to Christ where we are. We must be witnesses where we live, where we work, where we go to school, and where we spend our leisuretime. That is our world. If we don't win people where we are, then we certainly are not going to be effective in winning people where we aren't.

Let me put my finger on you. If people in your family are going to be converted, then it is up to you. If your schoolmates are going to be converted, it is up to you. If people where you work are going to be converted, it is up to you. We've got to do something to make ourselves available to God and to people. You say, "There are other people who can do it better than I." How many other people are burdened for the people you are burdened for? How many other people have the same circle of friends and interests that you do? You are unique, and the people you know and associate with are unique to you also. There are others who touch their lives but never in the same way you do.

If you are going to win people you know, then it is imperative that you be a good example. In fact, what the world needs is not more sales talks but more samples of the power of Jesus Christ. In one of the churches where I pastored, a man sold vitamins and health food for a living. He was the most emaciated, palest, and the most dried-up looking man I have seen in my life. He looked like death warmed over. I have seen mannequins in department store windows who looked more alive than he.

He came to me once and said, "Pastor, you need to be taking these vitamins and eating these health foods." I asked, "Do you take those vitamins? Do you eat that health food?" He replied proudly, "Yes, I do!" I said, "Then I don't want any."

If you are going to sell vitamins, then you had better have some vitality about your life. If you are going to sell health foods, you had better look and act healthy. How can I be impressed with your product if it apparently isn't helping you?

Our first responsibility as disciples is to live in such a way that we make Christianity contagious and appealing to other people. So what about your disposition? Your smile? Your attitude? If you are a critical, complaining, anxious, and uptight person, how can you ever influence anyone for Christ? If you go around criticizing the weather, your church, your company, and the country, who wants to be like that? On the other hand, if you have in your life peace, self-control, joy, purpose, and direction, other people will like what they see; they will want to know where you got it, and how much it will cost them.

Show people that Christ makes life better. If your life is boring, don't tell anybody that you are a Christian. If the only difference between you and other people is that you go to church one or two hours a week, then that is not enough difference to care about. People are already busy. They enjoy sleeping in too much on Sunday morning. If you can't show them more than that, then they won't be interested. If you laugh at the same jokes, have the same attitudes, are dominated by the same values, then nobody is going to be attracted to Christ.

The world doesn't expect us to be perfect, but it does expect us to be different. So, if you don't walk the walk, don't talk the talk.

Building Bridges of Love

Second, we represent Christ by what we do. Abraham Lincoln said, "People don't care how much you know until they know how much you care." If we want the world to be attracted to Christ, then we must be attractive not only in our attitudes but also in our actions.

If you want to reach people including members of your

family build a bridge of love to them. Remember them on their birthdays. Call them up occasionally. Write them notes. It is the little things that count. Keep the lines of communication open and the bridge of love in good repair. Mow your neighbor's yard, pick up his trash. Become all things to all men. In short, show them love and compassion and minister as Christ did.

The Bible makes this telling comment about Jesus' life, He "went about doing good" (Acts 10:38). That's one of the secrets of his effective witnessing. We are to do the same thing. The Bible says, "Let your light so shine before men, that they may see your good works, and glorify your Father which is in heaven" (Matt. 5:16). This is life-style evangelism. If people don't believe your words, they will at least be impressed by your works. It is a way of making contact with the lost world.

Whatever you do, you must be genuine—not a phony. Your love must be a sincere expression of Christ inside you. You can't fake it. You can't fool the world for long. After awhile people know what you really are.

It's Your Feel, Not Your Spiel

Third, you represent Christ by what you say. As important as your attitudes and your actions are, they are not enough by themselves. Living the Christian life is essential, but it is not all-sufficient. People may look at your life and know that it is different from theirs, and they may even want what you have, but they won't know why it is different, or where they can get it unless you tell them. How can you by the life that you live tell people that Christ died for their sins, was buried, and raised again on the third day? It just can't be done. To live your faith and never speak it is asking too much of you and too little of the gospel. If Jesus were to charge the church today in courtroom fashion he would charge us with malpractice of the mouth. We have not told others of Jesus Christ as we should.

Christianity is not difficult to communicate. It is simple. We make it hard by our extreme efforts. We give soul-winning courses that take six weeks to six months. This communicates to our people that winning others to Christ is extremely difficult.

As a result, Christians are scared to death to tell anybody about Jesus Christ. They memorize every possible question any non-Christian could ask as well as the correct answer: they want to have all of the bases covered. When they have done that, we say they are equipped. They aren't equipped; they are incapacitated. We have them so intent on nailing people with the Bible that they go out as unnerved as an elephant on ice.

How do you witness? What do you say to lost people? How do you share your faith? First, you give your testimony. That's simply telling people what has happened and what is happening in your own life right now. What has Christ done for you? Has he forgiven your sins? Are you at peace with your past because of his cleansing? Has he given you fulfillment? Has he enabled you to love those whom you did not love before? Has he brought you into a new circle of friends? Has he given your life meaning beyond yourself? Has he given you the calm assurance of the fact that you are mortal and that when you die you share in the hope of the resurrection? If so, tell other people about it. That's witnessing.

The marvelous thing about a testimony is that you can use it almost anywhere, people readily identify with it, and it has a note of authority about it. It does not need to be too polished. It needs only to be natural, simple, sincere, and believable. You are an expert at what God has done in your life. Tell somebody about it. It's your feel, not your spiel, that counts. Ernie Fritcher, a motivational speaker for General Motors said, "People are moved more by the depth of your conviction than by the height of your logic." So tell people what Christ has done for you.

Then share the gospel with them. In fishing terminology your testimony is the bait, and the gospel is the hook. What is the gospel? It is the power of God unto salvation. But what is it? We have all heard the gospel, but do we know what it is? If you came upon a wreck and a man was dying and you had to give him the gospel in just two or three sentences, what would you say? Don't say, "Matthew, Mark, Luke, and John." Don't even quote to him John 3:16. That is not the gospel. Paul gave us the gospel when he said, "For I delivered unto you first of all that which I also received, how that Christ died for our sins according to the scriptures; And that he was buried, and that he rose again the third day according to the scriptures" (1 Cor. 15:3-4).

That is the gospel. Christ died for our sins. Christ was buried. Christ was raised from the dead. It is this marvelous truth that can be used so effectively in winning people to Jesus Christ.

We are not bearing witness to the fact that we have arrived. We are not, as a church, saying to the world, "We have achieved perfection; come over here and be like we are." We are saying, "Look, we are here because we have acknowledged that we cannot go it on our own. We need God's grace and forgiveness and help. We have not arrived, but we have started." Our witness to Christ is that we have found someone who accepts us where we are and enables us to live with ourselves while he changes us. We have found in Christ someone who has given us real hope of being different. The world is hungry for this kind of authentic witness!

So keep your witness Christ centered. He is the Bread of life. He is the Water of life. He is the Light of the world.

He is the Good Shepherd. He is the One who reconciles us to God. He is the One who died for us. He is the One who can make people into new creatures. Keep focusing on Jesus Christ.

Then trust the Holy Spirit to convict. Remember the Holy Spirit is God's lawyer, and you are his witness. The Holy Spirit convicts the world of sin, righteousness, and the judgment to come (John 16:8-11).

When E. Stanley Jones, the great Methodist missionary, was a young man, he had studied in preparation to be a lawyer, then God called him to preach. In one of his first sermons, he decided to make a defense for Christ. And so, in very legal and technical form and language he prepared a brief concerning the life and ministry of Jesus Christ. As he presented his sermon the audience was unmoved and disinterested. As he came to the conclusion of it he closed his manuscript and said, "Let me close by sharing with you a few words of personal testimony concerning what Jesus Christ has done in my life." Then in the next two or three minutes he shared with his audience in a very personal, effective way, the power of Jesus Christ in his life. As he gave the invitation, people were greatly moved and responded to God's call. Later he remarked to a friend, "I failed as a lawyer for Christ. But I succeeded as a witness." That's what God wants out of us. He wants us to be his witnesses. The Holy Spirit is already working as his lawyer.

Very few people are ever converted by one witness. Usually it is an accumulation of experiences and witnesses that bring them to Christ. Most of us are just links in a chain that bring people to Christ. I would like to be the clenching link, but I can't always be. But I must be a witness and leave the door open for someone else to follow after me. I must not get into an argument and offend people so that no one else can come along and witness after me.

I have read the Bible from cover to cover for thirty years,

and I can't find anything in it which gives any physical specifications for being a witness for Christ. I can't find anything in the Bible which says that you are to be beautiful, young, educated, possessed of the great gift of oratory, or any other attributes but obeying the Great Commission. So let's do it.

It is not a sin to never have won another person to Christ. But it is a sin not to try. The Lord never demanded that we be successful. But he does demand that we be faithful. As disciples we are his witnesses, his ambassadors, and we must not forget it.

8. Caring for the Converts

Peter the Great, one of Russia's most famous csars, though great in size and influence on Russian history, was in many ways a man of humble spirit. When he set out to build Russia's first naval vessels, he hurled himself directly into the action. He slept in a small log house next to the shipyard and warmed himself by the same fires as his carpenters. Surrounded by the sound of ax, hammer, and mallet blows, he joined in the work as a common laborer.

In later months after his navy defeated the Turks, he joined his troops in a triumphant march into his capital city of Moscow. To the amazement of the Muscovites, instead of leading this glorious assemblage on a white horse or in a golden carriage at the head of his army, Peter walked with his troops behind his general's carriage, recognizable only by his great size.

With a desire to modernize Russia, he sent more than fifty Russians, most of them young sons of the noblest families, to western Europe to study seamanship, navagation, and ship building. These fifty were but the first wave. A "great embassy" would follow numbering more than two hundred fifty. The czar himself accompanied them. But he did not travel with the pomp and splendor of other heads of state. He traveled incognito as a mere member of the ambassador's staff.

Before his departure he had a seal engraved for himself. It bore the inscription: "I am a pupil and need to be taught."

That motto ought to characterize every one who is a disciple. We have already seen that the word *disciple* means "a learner." All disciples are pupils, and we should never lose our desire to be taught.

Most of us are where we are today largely because at some pivotal point in our life someone took time to teach us, train us, and mature us. Most often that someone was just an ordinary layman. In testimony meetings I have often asked people to tell about the person who has meant the most to them in their Christian life. Never once in twenty-eight years has anyone named a pastor. It has always been a parent, a godly aunt, or a grandmother, a Sunday School teacher, or a close friend. The reason for this is that pastors usually have responsibility for perhaps thousands of people. They touch many lives in a meaningful way but then move on to someone else. Usually those who have influenced us the most are those who spent a great deal of time with us over many years.

In my Christian experience, a cracker salesman named Elmer Nelson influenced me the most. He happened to be the coach of the church softball team that I played on as a boy. The fact that he was a softball coach is incidental. He could just as well have been a Sunday School teacher, a neighbor, an employer, or a close friend. Softball just happened to be the thing that brought us together. It was our point of contact. It enabled us to establish a relationship that blessed my life. Elmer loved me and had a special interest in me. After practice he would take me home, and we would sit in his car in front of my house, and he would talk to me about God, life, girls, and all the things that a father should talk to his son about. By the life that he lived and the words that he spoke, he actually discipled me without knowing it. I might well not be serving Christ today had it not been for the help he gave me in those formative years in my life.

In my denomination—Southern Baptist—there are over four million people who are nonresident church members. That means that at some time in the past these people made professions of faith and were baptized, but now we cannot locate them. Why is this? What happened to these people? In all probability we lost them because no one took time to follow up on them and to help them to grow, develop, and mature in their Christian life. The result is that they soon fell away.

It is the responsibility of every Christian to win others to Christ. But there should be no "dippin' and droppin' " of those we have won. It is our responsibility to disciple them. The Great Commission says that we are to be evangelists, but it also says that we are to be teachers.

Dr. James Kennedy in his book *Evangelism Explosion* writes, "Those who are merely satisfied with proclaiming the gospel and receiving professions are like immoral seducers. The seducer is satisfied merely to exploit and then tell of his exploits rather than enter into a meaningful marriage commitment."

We are not to exploit people but rather to help them to become all that God wants them to be. The apostle Paul is the greatest missionary-evangelist discipler who ever lived. In his writings we can see many of the follow-up methods he used. When he won people to Christ, he did not forget them, but rather he carried them on to Christian maturity. We should do the same.

One of Paul's first letters to new converts was the Book of 1 Thessalonians. That whole book in general and chapter 3 in particular helps us to see his primary follow-up techniques. Paul states in verse 10 that night and day he prayed exceedingly that he might be able to see these new believers face-to-face and "perfect" that which was lacking in their faith. The verb *perfect* means "to complete, to repair, to supply that which is lacking." Paul had led these people to a genuine faith in Jesus Christ, but their faith was not yet complete. It lacked the maturity it needed. So he wanted to add to that which they had already received and carry them on to Christian perfection. That was always his great goal for every believer.

In this chapter Paul either states explicitly or implies to us those follow-up techniques that he used so effectively. There are four of them: personal intercession, personal visitation, personal correspondence, and personal assignments.

Let's look at these four follow-up techniques, for they are things we ought to use ourselves in helping new converts.

The Nearest Way to Any Man

The first follow-up technique that Paul used was personal prayer. He knew that the nearest way to any man was through the heart of God. So he started every book he wrote in the New Testament except one with a prayer for believers. Those prayers are in the New Testament both to encourage us to pray for new converts and to give us an example of the specific things for which we ought to pray in the lives of others.

What did Paul pray for in the lives of these new Christians? There are three things he mentions specifically here. First, he prayed for God to direct their lives. Paul longed to see these Christians face-to-face, so he could help them grow in their Christian life. But he was having some difficulty in getting back to them; he prayed that the Lord would "direct" his way to them. If you are having a difficult time getting with someone that you need to nurture in the Christian life, why not pray about it? If the Lord is able to orchestrate the movement of the planets so that the whole universe works with such precision and harmony that we can set our watches by the movement of the planets, surely he can direct our lives to bring us in contact with the people we need to help.

Second, he prayed that their love for one another and for all men would increase and overflow. The final proof that we know him is that we love all men. So if we fail to love people, we are missing the essential ingredient of our Christian experience.

One first grade teacher sent home a report card with the notation: "Alvin excels in imagination, group integration, responsiveness, and activity participation. Now, if he could only learn to read and write." Imagination, group integration, and responsiveness are important. But reading and writing are essential. If a child does not learn the essentials, then he has failed in his education. Whatever else we do or leave undone in our Christian lives, if we do not love we are not what we ought to be.

At the outset of human history Cain asked, "Am I my brother's keeper?" (Gen. 4:9). There is no answer to that question in the Scriptures. But I will give you the correct answer. The answer is no. I am not my brother's keeper. I am not my brother's father. But I am my brother's brother.

The story of the good Samaritan helps me to see my duty as a brother and as a neighbor. I am called on to serve as a spiritual highway patrol on those roads that I travel. I have a responsibility for other people along life's way to love and to help them in times of need. If I miss out on love, then my faith will never grow to maturity. So we should ask God to increase our love for others.

Finally, Paul prayed that we would be steadfast in our holiness. It is scarcely possible to overestimate the value—potency—of the quiet, consistent, day-to-day living of a Christian layperson. Without this sustaining characteristic, whatever activity we may engage in is largely neutralized.

Before we become Christians, we have the nature of a pig. After we become Christians, we have the nature of a lamb. We are made for the Shepherd and his fold. It is inconceivable that a lamb would live comfortably in a pig-pen. A sheep may fall in the mud, but it will not wallow in it and enjoy it as a pig does. It has a different nature. If we are the children of God, we ought to live like it.

During World War II reporters sought out the sons of Theodore Roosevelt who were conducting themselves in a very splendid fashion in the european theatre of war. When congratulated one of them replied, "Well, after all, we are the sons of Roosevelt, and we must conduct ourselves correspondingly." As the sons and daughters of God redeemed by his grace in Jesus Christ, with hearts full of love and appreciation, we ought to live as the sons and daughters of God.

Do you pray for the members of your class? Your pastor and staff? Little children? Your neighbors? Paul in the Book of Romans mentioned twelve or thirteen people by name. He knew and prayed specifically for individuals. We should do the same. It is one of the surest ways to help people grow.

We ought to pray that God will bring us together in meaningful encounters. We ought to pray that God would cause our love for one another and the whole world to be increased. We ought to pray that God will strengthen us in holy living. This kind of praying helps people to mature.

We Learn Best by Association

The second method Paul used in follow-up was personal visits. In fact, his prayer was that God would make it possible for him to make a return visit to Thessalonica. In this chapter he repeatedly talked about things he had said when he was with them the first time, and the desire of his heart was to return once again (vv. 4,6,10-11).

This was Paul's pattern of work. He moved into a city, won people to Christ, established a church, and then moved on to another city. Later in his travels he would say to his companions, "Let's go back and strengthen the new converts." Then he would make return visits to deal with problems and help people continue to grow in the Christian life.

There are some things that are learned best by such personal contact. Early in my ministry I had a desire to be an effective personal witness for Christ. I had attended study courses, read books, and graduated from the seminary, but these did not teach me sufficiently.

So I began to invite pastors whom I knew to be effective personal witnesses to my church to preach revival meetings. As we went out visiting for the revival I would say to them, "I have already visited these people and talked to them about Christ. So this time, I want you to do the talking." As those men shared the gospel and their faith with these prospects, I made mental notes of what they were saying and how they said it. When I returned home, I jotted those notes down. I have them in my files until this day. Throughout the past twenty-eight years, I have used their same techniques, illustrations, and truths to present the gospel to countless thousands of people. What I could never have learned through reading books and taking courses, I did learn by personal contact and visitation with these effective men of God.

When people make decisions for Christ, we need to get with them and help them to begin to grow from the beginning. And we need to visit them again and again to see to it that they are well grounded in their new faith. Personal association with us will do as much to nurture them in the Christian faith as anything else we can do.

Power of the Pen

The third method Paul used in follow-up was personal correspondence. The entire Book of 1 Thessalonians is itself a testimony to this fact. Paul could not visit with the

Thessalonians personally, so he did the second best thing: he wrote them a personal letter. In fact, this letter and all the books of the New Testament are "follow-up" writings to new Christians. Did you know that the Gospel of Luke and the Book of Acts were both written to follow up on just one man? His name is Theophilus, and Luke wrote to ground him in the Christian faith (Luke 1:3; Acts 1:1)

In all of our craze over modern communications such as radio and television, we have forgotten the tremendous power of the pen. As someone has said, "A drop of ink can make a thousand think." If you listen to a message on the radio, and someone in the room coughs you may miss a crucial statement in that message. If you do, it is gone forever. If you are watching a religious service on television, and there is interference on the cable, then you may miss the thrust of the whole message. If so, it cannot be reclaimed. But if a message is written down with pen and ink it can be read, reread, pondered, laid down, and picked up again.

The Russians have a proverb that says, "What has been written with a pen cannot be hacked away with an ax." The writings of Christians like Aleksandr Solzhenitsyn have proven that to be true. All of the power of that mighty nation has not been able to stifle the work of God through their written words.

I still have in my possession the very first book that I ever owned. The home I grew up in didn't have any books in it whatsoever. Oh, my dad had a Masonic Bible, but he never read it. He kept it tucked away in a drawer somewhere. We did have a Sears and Roebuck catalog in our home which we read quite often. But there were no other books. The very first book I ever owned was *Christian Doctrine* by W. T. Conner. It was given to me on the occasion of my being licensed for the ministry. Could you guess who gave it to me? That's right: Elmer Nelson. He jotted a note in the flyleaf. It said, "Stay on the beam—we are behind you 100 percent." There is nothing eloquent about that statement. But it was a great encouragement to a boy who grew up in a non-Christian home and had little, if any, encouragement from his family. I knew that somebody was behind me, somebody cared.

He also wrote a Scripture under the note. It was 2 Peter 1:5-8. Here is what it says: "And beside this, giving all diligence, add to your faith virtue; and to virtue knowledge; And to knowledge temperance; and to temperance patience; and to patience godliness; And to godliness brotherly kindness; and to brotherly kindness charity. For if these things be in you, and abound, they make you that ye shall neither be barren nor unfruitful in the knowledge of our Lord Jesus Christ."

That passage has been a favorite of mine ever since. I've not yet added all of those virtues to my life, but I am still working on them.

Then on the back flyleaf of *Christian Doctrine,* Nelson wrote a poem. I'm not sure why he put it on the back flyleaf. Perhaps it was to see if I would read the book through.

Here is what he wrote:

> Just sitting and wishing,
>   Won't change your fate–
> The Lord provides the fishing,
>   But you have to dig the bait.

I've owned that book for over thirty years. And as you can imagine, it is a great treasure to me. It is a constant reminder of a person who loved me, kept up with me, and cared about me. When Elmer Nelson gave me that book, I was no longer on his softball team. He was still working with fourteen- and fifteen-year-olds. I was far beyond that then, but he had not forgotten me. He was still praying for me, visiting with me, and encouraging me.

It would be impossible to overestimate the impact of personal notes and letters people have written to me through the years. What an encouragement and help they have been to me. So if you want to have an impact on the lives of others, why not take the time to write them a personal letter of encouragement and admonition? They may very well remember that as long as they live. There are few things that you can do that will encourage people more than to personally correspond with them or, if you prefer, to give them a book that has been especially meaningful to you with a note of encouragement jotted in it. It is another way to help new converts to grow.

Delegate to Others

Paul's fourth method was to send a personal representative. As he grew older, Paul had won so many people to Christ and started so many churches that he could not keep up with all of them himself. But along the way he had trained men like Timothy and Titus and was able to delegate some of his follow-up work to them. He trained these men, trusted them, and gave them personal assignments. He encouraged Christians from the churches to receive them as his personal representatives and emissaries. Paul was always sending somebody to help out in the work of God. In this way he multiplied himself. We will look at the importance of multiplication in the next chapter.

Sending others to take your place can be effective, but it also has its drawbacks. I read once of a young man who fell in love with a young lady and planned to marry her. Just to show his love for her he decided to write her a postcard every day for an entire year. At the end of that year, she married the mailman.

Sending a representative is better than sending no one at all, but to go yourself is by far the best.

So it is a responsibility of every Christian to be both an

evangelist and a discipler. We are to busy ourselves about winning others to Jesus Christ, then to help them to grow to Christian maturity. G. K. Chesterton once said that whatever else a man is, he is not what he was meant to be. None of us are yet what we were meant to be. Even though we have received Christ as our Savior, we have not yet arrived. We will not be what we were meant to be until we become like Jesus Christ himself. He is the ideal man, the standard of perfection for every one of us. We must keep working, striving, and growing until we become like him.

Bernard Falk, the famous editor, wrote of the secret of the success of Lord Northcliffe. The secret was: "He was never satisfied."

I pray for you and for myself a holy restlessness. I pray that we will never be satisfied with our present growth or spiritual maturity, but that we will press onward and upward until we become everything that God wants us to be.

9. Christian Multiplication

It is important that we not only be disciples through commitment to Christ and that we make disciples through missions and evangelism, but we must also multiply disciples who in turn can make other disciples. That is the only way we will ever win our world to Christ.

There are more than a billion lost people in the world today. That's more people than most of us can comprehend. Let me put it another way to help you grasp the greatness of that number. If we were to line up all of the lost people in the world in one long line, that line would encircle the globe thirty times,—and it would grow twenty miles longer every day. If we then drove past all those people at a rate of fifty miles an hour for ten hours a day, seven days a week, it would take us four years and forty days to reach the place where we began; but by that time the line would be thirty thousand miles longer!

Or look at it another way. Picture two cars on an interstate highway leaving New York City headed toward Los Angeles, California. One car is traveling at the rate of 10 MPH, and the other is traveling at the rate of 100 MPH. The car traveling 100 MPH represents the expansion of the world population, and the car traveling 10 MPH represents the expansion of Christianity. Or let me put it yet another way. Stop all clocks at noon today, let time come to a standstill, lock all the cemeteries, close all the obstetric sections of hospitals. No one else is born or dies until the Southern Baptist Convention wins those now living to faith in Christ at its present rate of growth. At the rate we are baptizing people, it would take us about three-hundred years to win all the lost in America and over four-thousand years for us to win the rest of the world to Christ.

It seems clear to me that business as usual won't get the job done. If we are going to win our world to Jesus Christ we must start thinking in terms of multiplication, not just addition. We must not only be disciples, but we must also mature and multiply disciples who will in turn make and mature other disciples.

The potential for multiplication is astounding. If every person who is a Christian were to win one other person to Christ in the next six months, then each of those persons were to reach other persons, and those saved people were each to reach another person, in thirty-two years we would reach the entire population of the world for Christ. So, the possibilities of multiplication are staggering.

The Bible teaches that every disciple ought to be a multiplier. It is not enough for us just to be believers in Christ. It is not enough for us just to attend church. It is not enough for us just to be students of God's Word. God expects us to multiply ourselves in the lives of other people.

The principle of multiplication is clearly set out by both teaching and example in the Scriptures. Paul spoke of it when he wrote, "Therefore, my son, be strong in the grace that is in Christ Jesus. And the things that thou hast heard of me among many witnesses, the same commit thou to faithful men, who shall be able to teach others also" (2 Tim. 2:1-2).

There are four generations mentioned in these verses: Paul, Timothy, faithful men, and others. First, Paul was won to faith in Christ. Then he won and discipled Timothy. Now he encourages Timothy to multiply his ministry by training other faithful men who in turn would teach others.

Real discipleship involves both the reception and the

transmission of truth. To receive the word of God from another is a privilege. To transmit it to others is a responsibility.

If we take seriously this admonition from God's Word, then we must all assume a personal responsibility from the spiritual growth of other Christians. We must enter into an apprentice relationship with other Christians and pass on to them the things we have learned about the Lord, so they can do the same.

Our churches must not be primarily concerned about building an institution but about building people. We must not be concerned about groups only. We must also be concerned about individuals. Every person is important.

It is possible for us to become so numbers conscious that we fill our churches with empty people. This is not to discount the importance of numbers. We ought to be anxious to reach every person we can for Jesus Christ. But we must not lose sight of one individual in the great masses of people. Quality is as important as quantity. We must be concerned about taking every individual into a deeper walk with God, so they in turn may be disciple makers also.

Multiplying is one of the tests of our own discipleship. The test of a leader's effectiveness is not how many people follow him, but how many leaders he produces. The test of a Sunday School teacher's effectiveness is not how many pupils she has in her class, but how many teachers come out of that class. And the test of your discipleship is not how many verses you have memorized or how many tapes you have listened to or how many conferences you have attended, but how many disciples you have made.

If you are interested in being a discipler, here are three things that will help you. They are the three things that are essential to being a multiplier anywhere anytime.

First, you must enter into a close personal relationship with another person; second, you must encourage that person in his or her own commitment to Christ; and third, you must teach him what to teach others.

Discipleship Demands Relationship

The first thing necessary to being a multiplier is to develop a close personal relationship with another person. Discipleship demands relationship. The apostle Paul addressed Timothy as "my son." This is a term of endearment and suggests the close personal relationship that Paul had with Timothy. Timothy had been converted on Paul's first missionary journey. On his second journey, Paul saw the potential in Timothy and enlisted him as his assistant. In the years that followed, he accompanied Paul on his missionary journeys and learned not only from the teaching of Paul but also from the life of Paul. He learned by what he saw as well as from what he heard. In time Timothy became one of Paul's most dependable helpers. In those years, there developed such a close relationship between Paul and Timothy that Paul often spoke of him as his own son.

Timothy was not the only person with whom Paul had such a relationship. He had the unusal ability to establish meaningful relationships with others so as to be able to disciple them. In fact Paul often used parental terms in describing his close relationship to other believers. He called himself a nursing mother to the church at Thessalonica (1 Thess. 2:7). He speaks of himself as a spiritual father to the Corinthians (1 Cor. 4:15-16). He speaks of being in labor pains until Christ be formed in the believers of Galatia (Gal. 4:19). It was out of these close personal relationships that Paul did his discipling and his multiplying.

This was Jesus' method of reaching the world also. Jesus' ministry had both a public and a private aspect to it. In his public ministry Jesus preached, taught, and performed miracles among the masses.

But he also had a private ministry. His private ministry was building disciples. Jesus called his twelve disciples that they "should be with Him" (Mark 3:14). For three years Jesus shared his life and his ministry with these men in a close personal relationship. He spent three years as their school teacher, and school was never out. He was always teaching not only by what he said but by what he was and what he did. And when he ascended to the Father, those twelve were equipped to carry on his work of world evangelization.

Jesus did a lasting quality work in the lives of his disciples by developing a close personal relationship with them and spending quality time with them. If there had been a better way to do it, Jesus would have done it. We cannot improve on his plan; and he did it without radio, television, newspaper, printing press, or the automobile.

This kind of multiplication demands time. There is simply no way to multiply yourself through another person without spending time with him or her.

"But," you say, "I don't have time to spend with another person like that." You have the same amount of time that Jesus had. You have the same amount of time the president of the United States has. You have the same amount of time that anybody has. We always have time for things that are first in our lives. And multiplication should be a priority.

"Where," you ask, "can I find the kind of man that I need to disciple? The best place to find one is to win one to Jesus Christ yourself. That is what Paul did with Timothy. But you can also adopt somebody else's baby. That's what Barnabas did with Paul. Other people had a part in winning Paul to Christ, but they did not disciple him. It was Barnabas who took him under his wing and carried him on to Christian maturity. When the church at Jerusalem sent Barnabas to Antioch to supervise the work there, Barnabas immediately went to Tarsus to enlist Paul as his assistant

(Acts 11:22-28). For a whole year they worked together. Barnabas must have taught Paul much about loving people, getting along with people, and encouraging people. Barnabas literally poured his life into the apostle Paul. The end result was that Paul became the outstanding Christian leader of his day.

If you become a discipler, some of your disciples may outstrip you, as Paul did Barnabas, and become more effective in God's service than you. If so, thank the Lord you have succeeded in being a multiplier, find another person, and begin to work on that one. Paul would never have been the leader he was if Barnabas had not taken him under his wing for that year of specialized training.

If you want to be a multiplier, find a person who is anxious to grow in his understanding of and commitment to Christ. Meet with him on a regular basis, perhaps at breakfast once a week for prayer, Bible study, and sharing. Take him with you as you go out visiting for Christ. Teach her what you know and let her catch your spirit. And from the beginning make sure that in time she will be willing to do the same thing with someone else. Just be sure that you find you a faithful man or woman, one you can depend on. Some people are too caught up in their businesses and will not pay the price of discipleship. A good example of teachableness is Peter and the disciples fishing all night long and catching nothing. Then Jesus tells them to let down their nets on the other side of the boat, and they would catch a net full of fish. Remember now that this is Jesus, the carpenter, telling Simon, the fisherman, how to fish. But Peter was teachable. He obeyed the Lord, and God blessed him.

Don't waste your time on a carnal Christian who doesn't want to be discipled. It is easier to give birth to a new baby than it is to resurrect the dead. Get a new Christian or a hungry one who will respond, and get busy carrying him or her on in the Christian life.

Undergirded by Grace

The second thing necessary to being a multiplier is to encourage your person to grow in his own relationship to the Lord. Timothy needed to recognize that the source of his strength was in the Lord. It was not in himself. And it was not in Paul. It was in Jesus. So Paul encouraged Timothy to be strong in the grace that was in Christ Jesus (2 Tim. 2:1). Timothy's strength would come from the Lord, so he must stay close to him.

Where do we find grace? Where is it dispensed? Where is the getting place? The Book of Hebrews tells us to "come boldly unto the throne of grace, that we attain mercy, and find grace to help in time of need" (Heb. 4:14-16).

So there is a throne of grace available to us. And we approach that throne through prayer. Paul encourages Timothy to keep coming to God in prayer, so that he will find grace to sustain him in life.

The word *help* that is found in this Hebrews passage is the same word that is used to describe the girding of the ship the apostle Paul was on as he traveled to Rome. The ship was caught in a great storm and was about to be broken up by the waves when the sailors girded it with chains to keep it from breaking to pieces. As the chains held the ship together in the storm, so the grace of God holds us together in the storms of life.

What happens when we run low on grace? Why is it so important that we be strong in grace? Grace keeps us from cracking up under the pressures of life. It steadies us in the storms. When we run out of grace we run into trouble. We lose our tempers. We become critical. We become negative and discouraged. We lose our spiritual strength. We become selfish and hard to get along with. We cease to grow, witness, and disciple.

Inward strength for life is a loving gift from God. We must stay close to him to have strength for victorious living.

Teach Them What to Teach

The third thing necessary to being a multiplier is to teach your disciple what to teach someone else. Paul said to Timothy, "the things that thou hast heard of me among many witnesses, the same commit thou to faithful men, who shall be able to teach others also" (2:2). Paul taught Timothy what Timothy was to teach other people. Timothy was not to invent a new message. He was to teach the old one. We are to be transmitters of truth, not inventors of it.

This is not to minimize or depreciate the importance of study and of expressing your faith in a new and a fresh way. We must always beware of getting caught up in church dogma. Living by dogma is living by the conclusion of other people's thinking. While our faith was once and for all delivered unto the saints (Jude 3), every generation must rethink its faith and find fresh, new ways of expressing that faith to its world.

What did Paul teach Timothy? No doubt he taught him the whole of Christian truth. He must have taught him what any parent would teach his child—how to eat right, how to talk, how to walk, and how to share.

Every Christian must know how to eat right. If a person does not eat, he dies. Our spiritual food is the Word of God. Job said, "I have esteemed the words of his mouth more than my necessary food" (Job 23:12). So Paul taught Timothy to study the Scriptures (2 Tim. 3:16-18).

And, no doubt, he taught Timothy how to talk to God (1 Tim. 2:1-5), how to walk with God, and how to work for God. And he taught him how to share. As a child must be taught to be unselfish and to share with others, so Paul taught Timothy how to give (1 Tim. 6:17-18).

As you teach your disciple, you should also show her a

life that is worth copying. Many times Paul said, "Be followers of me." And he also said, "Our gospel came not unto you in word only, but also in power, . . . ye know what manner of men we were among you" (1 Thess. 1:5). Paul never hesitated to hold his own life up as an example for others. So you need to be the person you want your disciple to be. Let him hear the truth from your lips, and let her see it in your life, and it will make a difference.

All of this needs to be done in the context of evangelism. If all you are doing with your disciple is studying the Scriptures and having prayer, then you'll have good fellowship, but you won't have any fruit. There won't be another one reached for Christ. The ultimate goal of all that we do is to win others to Christ, so they can be discipled to win other people to Christ also. You will never have any spiritual grandchildren unless you make a disciple who in turn wins someone else to Christ. It takes a disciple to build a disciple. But discipleship is not complete until you have reached out in evangelism.

Christianity is just one generation from extinction. If Paul doesn't work with Timothy or Timothy doesn't work with someone else, that's the end of the line. There is no progress beyond that. Let us sit idly by and not reach out to evangelize, and Christianity comes to a full stop.

Paul's admonition to Timothy was that he "commit" the things that he had learned to faithful men who would in turn teach others also (1 Tim. 2:2). The word *commit* is a banking term. It means "to make a deposit" or "to entrust for safe keeping." There are three commitals in 2 Timothy (2 Tim. 1:12; 1:14; 2:2). In the first instance, Paul speaks of having committed his salvation to the Lord. In the second instance he speaks of the Lord having committed his Word to us. In the last instance he speaks of our committing what we have learned to faithful men that they may teach others also.

The first commitment makes you a Christian. The second commitment makes you a witness. The third commitment make you a disciple. The first commitment is a commitment of salvation. The second commitment is a commitment of evangelization. The third commitment is a commitment of multiplication. Which of these three commitments represents you?

Christian, witness, multiplier—that's what every disciple is to be.

10. Disciples in Difficult Places

The Christian life, someone has said, does not get easier, but it does get better. I can testify to the truthfulness of both parts of that statement. The Christian life does get better. As the songwriter says, "Every day with Jesus is sweeter than the day before." But it is equally true that the Christian life does not get easier.

Age does not make it easier. I am not finding it easier to live for Christ at the age of forty-eight than I did at the age of eighteen. To be sure the problems I face are different, but they are just as intense. Age makes no difference.

Location does not make it easier to serve Christ. I do not find it easier to live for Christ in Tyler than I did in San Marcos or in Taylor or in Troy or in any other place I have lived. And my vocation does not make it any easier. The fact that I am a minister does not make it easier for me to live for Christ than anyone else. We ministers have the same weaknesses, temptations, desires, and struggles as everyone else. Does that surprise you? There are some people who think that we preachers are so holy that we take nothing but Saint Joseph's aspirin. The fact of the matter is that we take Excedrin II just like other Christians and sometimes because of them.

While it is always difficult to be a disciple, it is never impossible. Regardless of your age, your geographical location, or your vocation, you can live for Jesus Christ. Even in the hardest of places and in the most unlikely surroundings people have, and still do, live for him. A verse that assures us of this was written by the apostle Paul to the Philippian Christians when he said, "All the saints salute you, chiefly they that are of Caesar's household" (Phil. 4:22). Paul was incarcerated in a Roman prison when he wrote these words. The church at Philippi had learned of his imprisonment and had sent a personal representative along with a love offering to help him in his work. In response to their gift Paul wrote this letter. In addition to his own greeting he ends the letter with a greeting from all the Christians in Rome, especially those saints who lived in Caesar's household.

There are three words in this verse that need some examining. The first is the word *saint.* What or who is a saint? A saint is not a statue of stone placed in a cathedral. The word *saint* is a synonym for a Christian. A Christian is a saint, and a saint is a Christian. They are one in the same. The word *saint* actually refers to a person who has been set apart for God and his service. So the saints that Paul referred to here are real live people who had committed themselves to Jesus Christ and are seeking to live for him.

These saints were living in an unusual place. They were saints in "Caesar's household." The word *household* refers to either a family or a home. These saints were not necessarily blood relatives of Caesar. In all probability they were members of his civil service or a part of his praetorian guard or they were slaves who served in his palace.

Caesar was the emperor of the Roman Empire. Caesar at this time was Nero Claudius Caesar. He was one of the cruelest and most wicked men who ever lived. He killed his own mother. He murdered his own wife. And he had his halfbrother put to death. He was so evil that when he died the citizens of Rome danced for joy in the streets. Near the end of his fourteen-year reign, Nero turned against the Christians. He burned the city of Rome and blamed it on them. In a public display of outrage he impaled Christians on stakes, covered their bodies with pitch, then set them on fire, and used them as human torches to light his gardens. He covered Christians with fresh animal skins and turned his wild dogs loose on them just for the joy of seeing them torn to pieces.

Can you imagine a harder place to be a saint than in Caesar's household? To live for Christ under the nose of this cruel and despicable man who hated Christianity must have been extremely difficult. Yet the apostle Paul sends this greeting from some Christians who were doing just that.

There is a message in this for you and for me. It is this: if a person could be a disciple in Caesar's household, then one can be a disciple anywhere. If it was possible to be a Christian in that place, then it is possible to be a Christian any place.

The truth of this message is that if there could be saints in Caesar's household, there can be saints anywhere in the world. Those hard places like Caesar's household are the arena of discipleship. Anyone can be a disciple in a monastery. Anyone can be a Christian in a stately cathedral. Anyone can be a follower of Christ at a religious camp. But to be a Christian in everyday life—that is the hard thing to do, and that is the real test of our discipleship.

There are at least four places where it is especially difficult to be a disciple today. I want us to look at those places with the understanding that if a person could be a disciple in Caesar's household, then we can be a disciple in these places also. The four places where it is hard to live for Christ today are: schools we attend, social circles we move in, businesses we work in, and the houses we live in.

Disciples at School

It is hard for young people to live for Christ today. Several things make this so. Three of them are: the moral confusion of our age, excessive freedom, and peer pressure. We are living in a time of unprecedented moral confusion. The prevailing moral philosphy in today's America is, "If it feels good, do it." Occasionally, I drive up behind some people who are stopped at a traffic light, and they have a bumper sticker on their car that reads: "If it feels good, do it." Usually, it is a pickup truck with a shaded back window and a few beer cans lying around in it. When I see that bumper sticker, I feel like putting my car in reverse, backing off about thirty feet, and then ramming them so hard that I knock them halfway across the intersection. Then if they jumped out of the truck and asked me, "Why did you do that?" I would reply, "Because I thought it would feel good." With many people in America today what is right is what they feel good after, and what is wrong is what they feel bad after.

People have always violated moral standards. But for the first time in the history of the world, many people are not even sure that there is such a thing as an absolute moral standard. Then you add to the moral confusion of our age excessive freedom, and the problem is compounded. With the freedom that comes from affluence and a lack of responsibility, people are bored; thus they are looking for new thrills and excitement. In fact, let me give you a foolproof formula for boredom. Too many things plus too much leisure plus too few responsibilities equals boredom. If you take morally confused people who are bored with life and add to that the peer pressure of "everybody's doing it," then you've got the mess we are in today.

I am persuaded that it is harder to live for Jesus Christ in the public schools and in the universities today than it has ever been before in the history of the world. But as difficult as it is, it is not impossible. If there could be saints in Caesar's household, there can be saints in our public schools and our universities. But there is a price to be paid. It requires a deep commitment to Jesus Christ and his Word. We cannot survive the pressures of today without being anchored to him.

Robert W. Young illustrated this truth by the use of a violin string he had on his desk. The string was not attached to anything. It was free. But it was not free to do what a violin string is supposed to do—produce music. So he attached the string to the base of the violin, ran it up the neck, attached it to one of the keys, and twisted the key until the string was taut. Only then was it capable of producing beautiful music. It was only after it was attached and fastened down that it could do what a violin string is supposed to do.

The same thing is true with your life and mine. Absolute freedom is absolute nonsense. It leads to complete frustration and emptiness. It is only as we attach our lives to Jesus Christ that we can ever fulfill our intended purpose. It is only through commitment to him that our lives can produce the beautiful melody that God wants to come from them. In spite of all the difficulties and hardships that you may find in living for Jesus Christ in your school today, it can be done. If there were saints in Caesar's household, then it is possible that there can be saints among young people today.

The Social Swirl

The social circles we move in are also hard places to be a disciple. Young people aren't the only ones who face social pressures. Adults also know what it is to be tempted to conform and to compromise—to go along in order to get along. Somebody has said that every person is born an original and dies a copy. Life is often a gradual process of whittling away our distinctiveness until we are all just alike.

Many Christians today are like the chameleon. A chameleon, you know, is a lizard that changes its color to match its environment. That is a part of its defense mechanism. A little boy was playing with a chameleon one day; he put it on a piece of bark, and it turned brown in color. Then he took it off the bark and put it on a leaf, and it turned green in color. Then he put it back on the bark, and it turned brown again. Then he put it back on the leaf, and it turned green again. He repeated this action over and over until finally he put the chameleon on a piece of plaid cloth, and it had a nervous breakdown.

There are lots of chameleon Christians today. They are so busy trying to conform to the world around them that they live in nervous exhaustion. They have forgotten the admonition of the apostle Paul that we be not conformed to this world (Rom. 12:1-2).

While it is hard to live for Jesus Christ in the social swirls of our communities, it is not impossible. Listen! If there could be saints in Caesar's household, there can be saints at the country club. In fact, if you can't live for Christ at the country club you need to get out. Your first calling is to be a saint. It is to live for Jesus Christ. It is not to conform to the image of the world around you.

The favorite motto of Samuel Adams, the great American patriot, was, "Take a stand from the start, lest by one concession after another you end up in complete subjection." Adams was talking about political and international affairs, but what he said also applies to our social lives. Very few Christians jump into sin. We either slip or drift slowly into it, almost imperceptibly. We don't intend for it to happen; it just happens before we know it. We make first one little concession and then another; before we are aware of it, we are caught like a fly in a spider's web.

It will take many ages to surpass the simple wisdom of Aesop's fables. One of these fables especially relates to this point. A woodman came into a forest to ask the trees to give him a handle for his ax. It seemed so modest a request that the principal trees at once agreed to it, and it was settled among them that the homely ash would be sacrificed to furnish the handle. No sooner had the woodmen fitted the handle into the blade of his ax than he began felling trees all about him on all sides, even the noblest trees in the forest. The oak, now seeing the consequences, said to the cedar, "The first concession has lost all; if we had not sacrificed our humble neighbor, we might have stood yet for ages ourselves."

Take a stand from the start. Don't make the first concession in your social life. Let people know what you believe and where you stand. You don't have to do that in a brash, haughty, self-righteous sort of way. There is no place for that in the Christian life. If we become self-righteous, then we are worse in spirit than others are in practice. We can walk to the beat of a different drummer, we can live our lives on a higher plane, and we can be committed to Christ in our social lives. If there could be saints in Caesar's household, there can be saints anywhere.

Business Is a Hard Place

Another place where it is hard to be a disciple today is in the business world. It is hard to live for Christ there because many people check their Christianity at the door when they go to work. When they punch in for work, they punch out for Christ.

Many people believe that Christianity was intended only for clerical collars, choir robes, and stately cathedrals. But the truth of the matter is that it was meant for the smoke-filled office, the mechanic's shop, the construction site, and the cab of an eighteen-wheeler. In fact, Christianity looks best when it is dressed in blue denims, a mechanic's overalls, and a housewife's apron.

"But," some of you will say, "You don't understand how they talk where I work," "You don't understand what goes on among men and women in our office," Or "You don't understand how materialistic my boss is."

I probably understand much better than you think. But even if I didn't, I know this: if there could be saints in Caesar's household, then a person can be a Christian where you work. If these saints could live for Jesus Christ in the hardest of all places, surely you can live for Jesus Christ at your place of employment. It is simply a matter of commitment. If you want to live for Christ, then you can.

We need to look at our work as William Carey, the founder of the modern mission movement, looked at his. William Carey was a shoe cobbler by profession when God called him to be a preacher and a missionary. Thereafter, he said about his work, "My job is to preach the gospel; I cobble shoes to pay expenses." It would be wonderful if every Christian saw his primary responsibility as preaching the gospel of Christ. Then we could all say, "My job is to preach the gospel. I work in the law office just to pay expenses." Or "My job is to preach the gospel. I sell insurance just to pay expenses." Or "My job is to preach the gospel. I am a secretary just to pay expenses."

There is no higher calling than to devote your life to the spread of God's Word. If you will see your work in that light, it will transform both you and your work. Your work will no longer be a drudgery. You will suddenly become concerned about both the quality and the quantity of your work. For even the way you do your work will be a means of preaching God's Word to those who do not believe it or practice it.

I am convinced of this: if there could be saints in Caesar's household, there can be saints where you work also.

Being a Disciple at Home

John Bunyan once described some people as being saints abroad and devils in the home. There are people who greet strangers with a sweet hello and a friendly smile, but in their own homes they speak in the sharpest and ugliest of ways.

Why wouldn't this be true? After all, our home is the one place where it is hardest to live for Christ, for it is the one place where we are really ourselves. When we go out we not only put on our best clothes, but we also put on our best manners. When we are out in public we not only try to look our best, but we try to act our best. What we are in the home is what we really are down deep inside. Much of what we are at other times and in other places is nothing more than a charade.

We all need the resolve of David who said, "I will walk within my house with a perfect heart" (Ps. 101:2). You say, "But you don't know what it is like in my house. You don't have to live with a woman like my wife." Or "You don't have to live with an old grouch like my husband." Or "You don't know how unreasonable my parents can be." Or "You don't realize how rebellious my kids are." No, I may not realize all of those things, but I know this: if there could be saints in Caesar's household, then there can be saints in your household also. If people could live for Christ in Nero's palace, then they can live for Christ in your house, too.

There are at least three things that are necessary if we are to live for Christ in our homes. The first is love. The Scriptures teach that husbands are to love their wives as Christ loved the church, and that wives are to love their husbands. There is nothing more important to building a good home than a husband loving his wife, a wife loving her husband, parents loving their children, and children loving their parents. There can be no Christian home without Christian love.

The second ingredient of a Christian's home is teaching. In the Old Testament the Jews were told that they should teach their children the Word of God when they got up in the morning, when they sat in their houses, when they traveled on a journey, and when they lay down at night (Deut. 6:7). In all of the normal events of life, they were to teach and train their children. The most effective teaching does not take place when you say to your child, "Sit down and be quiet! I am going to tell you a thing or two." The most effective teaching takes place simply by living together. As we walk together, work together, sit together, we teach and transmit the true values of life.

The final thing necessary for a Christian home is example. Gipsy Smith, the evangelist, once said, "There are really five gospels. There is The Gospel According to Matthew, The Gospel According to Mark, The Gospel According to Luke, The Gospel According to John, and the gospel according to you." Which gospel do you think your children learn best while they are living at home? Long before they are able to recite their *ABC*s or are able to read the other four Gospels, they are reading the gospel according to us. If we can give them the right kind of example, the time will come when they will look on that example and say, "That's what I really want in my life." Then they will almost invariably turn back to God if they have drifted away from him.

R. G. Lee once told of a young boy who was seriously ill and going to die. The doctor felt that the boy needed to be told of his approaching death, and the responsibility for telling him fell on the shoulders of his own father. As they talked together one day, the boy asked his father, "Dad, how am I doing?" And the father replied, "You are not going to get well, my son; you are going to die." "But," he said, "Son, I want you to remember this: when you die you are going to be with Jesus." The boy looked into the face of his father and said, "Dad, if Jesus is anything like you, I don't mind going."

Every child needs this kind of example. Living for Christ in the home is seldom easy. But as difficult as it may be, it can be done. If there could be saints in Caesar's household, there can be saints in your household also. ⟋

Several years ago I led a tour group to Israel. Our guide was an attractive and intelligent young Jewish girl named Ruthie. She had majored in archaeology and history in college, and she literally made the Bible lands come alive to us. One night some of our people were talking with her about the place of the Jews in history. Then someone said to her, "You know, Ruthie, you Jews are the people of God." She said, "Yes, I know. And I wish we weren't; it's such a terrible responsibility."

Listen! If you are a disciple, you are one of God's children. You have been adopted into his family through faith in Jesus Christ. And that is an awesome responsibility. It is imperative that we live like it. We need to be saints at the school we attend, in the social circles we move in, in the places where we work, and in the homes where we live.

There are some places where it is very difficult to be a disciple. But there is no place where it is impossible. We can live for Christ in those hard places. They are the arena of Christian discipleship.

11. Lordship and Discipleship

The name of Jesus is not so much written in history as it is plowed into it. One evidence of this is the fact that historian Arnold Toynbee devoted more space to Jesus of Nazareth than to any other six men combined who have ever lived including Muhammad, Buddha, Caesar, Napoleon, and George Washington.

This fact is even more remarkable when we know that Toynbee was not a Christian himself. He was an atheist. The reason he gave Jesus this place of prominence in history was that his influence demanded it. When any objective historian considers the number of books that have been written, the number of songs that have been composed, the number of buildings that have been built, the number of services that have been conducted, and the amount of progress that has been made in the name of Jesus, one must admit that Jesus is the most significant person who has ever lived in the history of the world. No other person has had in the past or still has in the present as profound an influence upon humanity as Jesus.

Why is this? How can we account for the impact of Jesus on the world? It is the fact that Jesus Christ is Lord. The word *Lord* is the most common title for Jesus in the New Testament. If I were to ask an average Christian today, "Who is Jesus?" he or she would probably say that Jesus is the Savior. However, the New Testament more often speaks of him as Lord. Jesus is called Savior 24 times in the New Testament. And he is called Lord 433 times.

What does it mean to call Jesus Lord? The Greek word translated Lord is *kurios*. It had several meanings. It was the normal title of respect used by a slave for his master. It was also the accepted title of honor for the emperor of the Roman Empire. And it is the Greek translation of the revered Hebrew name for God, Jehovah. So when a Jewish convert said "Jesus is Lord," he meant that Jesus was his God. When a Roman convert said "Jesus is Lord," he meant that Jesus, not Caesar, was his King. And when a slave said "Jesus is Lord," he meant that Jesus was his Master and owner.

The confession "Jesus is Lord" was the initial confession of the church; it is the essential confession of a Christian, and it will be the eventual confession of all creation. Because of who Jesus is and what he has done, God has made his name the most important name in time and in eternity. Eventually, every knee in heaven and on earth and even in hell itself shall bow before Jesus, and every tongue shall confess that he is Lord (Phil. 2:9-11).

It is essential to confess Jesus as Lord in order to be a Christian. We must believe in our hearts and confess with our mouths the fact that Jesus is Lord if we are to be saved (Rom. 10:9-10).

And the confession "Jesus is Lord" was also the initial confession of the church. In the first Christian sermon delivered on the Day of Pentecost Peter declared, "Therefore let all the house of Israel know assuredly, that God hath made that same Jesus, whom ye have crucified, both Lord and Christ" (Acts 2:36).

What is the evidence that Jesus is really Lord? How can we be sure that he is more than just a man? What is there to substantiate the theme of Peter's preaching? At the beginning of his sermon Peter gave four evidences of the lordship of Christ. They were the miracles, wonders, and signs that he did (v. 22), his resurrection from the grave (v.

31), his ascension into heaven (v. 33), and finally, the outpouring of his spirit on the world (v. 33). The proof then that Jesus is Lord is his wonderful miracles, his triumphant resurrection, his glorious ascension, and the mighty working of his Spirit in our world today.

On the basis of these things, everyone can know with absolute certainty that Jesus Christ is Lord. It is this fact—the lordship of Christ—that is the basis of our discipleship. It is because Jesus is Lord that we worship him, obey him, follow him, serve him, and learn of him.

What does the lordship of Christ mean to us today? When we call Jesus "Lord" we are saying that he is the God we worship, the King we obey, and the Master we serve. It means that we give Him the loyalty of our lives, the worship of our hearts, and the control of our will.

God Became Flesh

The essence of Christianity is this: Jesus is God. He is not just a part of God; he is not just sent from God; he is not just related to God; he was and is God. This is the message that turned the Roman Empire upside down in the first century.

The early Christians faced the severest kind of persecution, not because they plotted to overthrow the Roman government or because they denounced the evils of slavery or because they protested the excessive taxes of Rome but because they proclaimed that Jesus Christ was God.

The Jews who heard their message believed that Jehovah was God. The Romans who heard their declaration believed that Jupiter and Mercury were gods. But they did not believe that the lowly carpenter of Nazareth was God.

John declared the central truth of the gospel when he wrote, "The Word was made flesh, and dwelt among us" (John 1:14). Michelangelo expressed himself in marble. Sir Christopher Wren expressed himself in granite. Joseph

Turner expressed himself in oils. Handel expressed himself in music. Shakespeare expressed himself in ink. And God expressed himself in flesh.

What is more expressive than flesh? The twinkle of an eye, a smile of the lips, a rosy cheek, a warm handshake—all are superexpressive. Jesus is God in flesh getting down to my level so that I can understand him.

If persons tried to express themselves to me in Japanese, they would not get very far. That is a foreign language to me. I don't understand it. Neither would God get far in expressing himself to me in celestial language. However, since God expressed himself to me in flesh, I can com-, prehend him. That's what I am. I understand flesh. That is where I live.

Since Jesus is God, he deserves to be at the very center of our lives. Think of your life as a wheel. A wheel has three parts: a rim, spokes, and a hub. It is the same with our lives. The rim represents the circle of influence that we have. The spokes represent the various interests of our lives such as our work, our school, our recreation, our family, and our friends. And the hub represents the stabilizing force of our lives. Jesus as God ought to be the hub of our lives. He ought to be the very center of our being. As a wheel without a hub would collapse or wobble out of control, so our lives without Jesus Christ are more likely to collapse under the pressures of daily living. Without him, we lack what psychiatrists call "an integrated life."

G. K. Chesterton once said that it is often supposed that when people stop believing in God, they believe in nothing. But, alas, it is worse than that. When they stop believing in God, they believe in anything. The denial of God brings the death of authority. And the death of authority brings the birth of anarchy and confusion.

Jesus as Lord holds the universe together. "By him all things consist," Paul declared (Col. 1:17). If he can hold the galaxies of space in their orbit, then surely he can keep our lives from falling to pieces when we make him our Lord.

Jesus Is Chief

In the first century world Caesar, the emperor of the Roman Empire, held absolute power over both men and nations. Into that world the disciples came proclaiming that there is another king: King Jesus (Acts 17:7). He alone, they said, was worthy of a person's highest allegiance and greatest devotion. That message, "Jesus is King," helped to turn the New Testament world upside down.

Jess Fletcher in his book *Wimpy Harper of East Africa* tells that toward the end of his second year in Nigeria, Wimpy took a ten-mile trek on his cycle through the desolation that characterizes the Nigerian countryside.

A school teacher and a pastor, both Nigerians, were with him. The village to which they were going had never had a visit from a missionary before. When they arrived, Wimpy arranged to salute the king. To his relief, he found the chief friendly.

"You are the first missionary to visit our village. We are honored," the king said softly and courteously.

"I am honored to visit your town," Wimpy said, "and to salute the chief. Your hospitality is most gracious."

"Once before white men came to our town," the chief said with a twinkle in his eye. "They were looking for elephants. What are you looking for?"

"I am come to tell your people of the King of kings and of his power to cleanse a man from his sins and to make him whole again."

"A King of kings?" replied the chief, his interest aroused.

By now the king had exhausted his English, and they were communicating through Pastor Oyezmi. Through the pastor Wimpy told the chief of Jesus and his power to save the vilest sinner.

After a time the king said, "If I thought I could give up my sins, I would gladly receive Jesus." Wimpy was almost caught off balance by the sudden development. He was no longer just telling the chief about his mission; the chief was deeply interested and under conviction of his own need. Earnestly and hardly realizing that he was speaking through an interpreter, Wimpy told the chief that Jesus would take away his sins if he would trust him to do so. Jesus would also give him power to give up his sins. He did not have that power within himself. The moment was charged with the dramatic picture of an earthly monarch facing a heavenly one.

Haltingly, the chief said, "I will accept Jesus as my Lord."

Wimpy asked him to kneel and trust himself to Jesus Christ and to thank God for his salvation. The old chief arose from his throne and stepped to the ground. There, helped by his right-hand man, he knelt to the ground to the amazement of those who watched wordlessly. He bowed his head and prayed in words that Wimpy could not understand but in a tone of voice that rang true. Later Pastor Oyzemi said that the chief had prayed for himself, his family, and his village.

Now the chief looked up at Wimpy and his friends. Slowly he reached up and took his crown from his head. He said, "Now, Jesus is my chief."

To confess Jesus as Lord is to say that he is the Chief of your life. And as the Chief or King, he should rule and reign in every part of it. Imagine your life, this time not as a wheel but as a house. The library represents your mind, the control room of your life. The dining room represents your appetites. The den represents your social relationships. The workshop represents your hobbies and your recreation. And the closets represent the hidden things of your life. When you make Jesus the Lord of your life, you should give him the "master key" to it and authorize him to have the run of the whole house. No part of your life should be shut off from his presence and his control. Your thoughts, your appetites, your friendships and your relationships, your activities and your hobbies, and even the hidden things of your life should be brought under his control.

If you will let him, Jesus will enter into every part of your life and control it and enrich it. Sam Jones said, "Christ always lives where there is room for him. If there is room in your heart for Christ, he lives there; if there is room in the law office for Christ, he lives there; if there is room on the locomotive engine, he lives there; if there is room in the baggage car, he lives there."

To confess Jesus as Lord is to make him the King of your life.

Jesus Is Master

The New Testament world into which the gospel first went was riddled with slavery. People bought and sold other people as though they were cattle or sheep. They owned them and their families lock, stock, and barrel. They exercised absolute authority over them—having the power of life and death in their hands. The word *master* that was used to describe a slave owner also means Lord. To confess Jesus as Lord then means that he is our Master and our owner, and we are his slaves.

I once talked to a college student about becoming a Christian. He was interested in salvation, but he said that he did not want to attend church every Sunday. He said, "I want to worship when I please and pray when I please." I pointed out to him that when he became a Christian, his life would be under new management. He would then be owned by Jesus Christ, and his supreme desire and responsibility would be to please the Savior (2 Tim. 2:3).

It is true that when we become Christians we are no longer our own. We belong to him (1 Cor. 6:19-20). Our bodies, our talents, our time, our money, our home—everything belongs to him. Jesus Christ is Lord; he is Master; he is Owner.

The essence of sin is to reject Jesus as Master. Jesus once told the story of a certain rich man who planned a trip into a distant land. So he called in his ten servants and trusted his wealth to them to be managed for him while he was gone. No sooner had he left the country than the citizens of that country sent him a message that said, "We will not have this man to reign over us" (Luke 19:14).

In this parable the nobleman represents Christ. The response of the people, "We will not have this man to rule over us," represents the hardened, calloused, sinful attitudes of people.

Sin is not just drunkenness, adultery, divorce, or dishonesty. Sin is the refusal to allow Jesus Christ to be the Lord and Master of your life. Do you see Jesus as the legitimate owner of your life? Have you surrendered your will to him? Are you seeking to obey his every command?

To allow Jesus to rule over us is not irksome; it is liberating. The apostle Paul declared this marvelous truth when he said, "From henceforth let no man trouble me: for I bear in my body the marks of the Lord Jesus" (Gal. 6:17). The "marks" that Paul referred to were brand marks used by masters on their slaves. Slave owners often branded their slaves in the same way that our forefathers branded their cattle. In case they ran away, they could easily be identified by these brand marks and returned to their rightful owner. Paul compared the scars that he had received in missionary service to the brands placed on slaves by their owners. He was saying in essence, "Christ is my Master; these scars are his brand marks to prove that I belong to him."

Behind this statement was the fact that Paul was being

severely criticized by some people. He wanted them to understand that because Jesus was his Lord, he was free from being a slave to their opinions and criticism. He no longer wanted to be bothered by it. Since Jesus was his Lord, his only concern was to please him. What others thought of him, therefore, was not a major concern of his. So they need not bother him with their criticisms or their complaints any more. Having Jesus as his Lord set him free from all other masters. It can do the same for you also. What a relief for a Christian worker to be set free from the slavery of what others think of him and to be able to live only to please the Lord.

Every Christian leader from Moses until the present has encountered criticism and resistance. Any Christian leader who is to survive and not become paranoid must eventually decide who his master is. We must not be so naive as to believe that everybody will like our leadership. But if we know whom we work for we can be relatively free from feeling that we have to please everyone or have everybody like us. In fact, we should be disappointed if some people like us. Some people do not want to do anything. Some people are looking for a religion of convenience. Some people want a cold, stiff, formal church. We should be disappointed if such people really like us. Jesus is our Master. It is enough if he is pleased with us.

Jesus is Lord; therefore, all of us should surrender ourselves to him and become his disciples. In fact, his lordship is the basis of our discipleship. It is because of who he is and what he has done that we honor him, follow him, and learn of him.

I read once about a drifter who came across a man who was preparing to shoot a dog. "Say," said the drifter, "why are you going to shoot that dog?"

"Mister," said the man, "this dog's name is Gypsy. He

follows everybody's wagon, and any dog that follows everybody's wagon is no good to anybody."

"Mister," said the wanderer, "would you let me have that dog?"

"I guess so, but he's no good."

The drifter tucked the little dog under his arm, threw his duffel bag over his shoulder, and moved on. As he walked along he said to the dog, "Gypsy, you and I are two of a kind. I've been a Christian a long time, but I have followed after everybody's wagon. I've given allegiance first to this person and then to that one and sometimes to the Lord. You've helped me to see how foolish all this is. From now on, we are going to change things. I'm going to be your master, and Christ is going to be mine."

Oh, that this might be true in all our lives. It can be. And it all begins when we accept Jesus as Lord.

When Peter had finished his first sermon declaring Jesus as Lord, his hearers cried out, "What shall we do?" Peter answerd, "Repent, and be baptized" (Acts 2:37-38). To become a Christian you must make an about-face in your thinking concerning Jesus Christ. You may have thought that Jesus was just a man. You may have thought that Jesus was a common criminal. You may have thought that Jesus was simply a great teacher. But now you must recognize him as Lord. He is the God you are to worship; he is the King you are to obey; He is the Master you are to serve. Then you should openly acknowledge your allegiance to Christ by being baptized. This is the way to God. This is the way of salvation. This is the way of discipleship.

12. The Secret of Dynamic Discipleship

Jesus came that we might have life and have it more abundantly. The abundant life is a life of joy, peace, fulfillment, meaning, and victory. However, very few of God's people experience a quality of life that deserves to be called "abundant." In fact, I would estimate that 90 percent of the Christian people I know are living defeated, frustrated, and discouraged lives. Why is this true? It is because they are trying to live the Christian life in their own strength. They have been saved by the grace of God. Their sins have been forgiven. They have been adopted into the family of God. And they are on their way to heaven. But in the meantime they are trying as hard as they can in their own power to live the Christian life. This is an impossible situation, so they find themselves defeated and frustrated.

Every disciple faces the danger of trying to grow to maturity and serve Christ in the flesh. The secret of victorious living is implied in a series of carefully worded questions which the apostle Paul asked of the churches of Galatia. He asked, "O, foolish Galatians, who hath bewitched you, that ye should not obey the truth, before whose eyes Jesus Christ hath been evidently set forth, crucified among you? This only would I learn of you, Received ye the Spirit by the works of the law, or by the hearing of faith? Are you so foolish? having begun in the Spirit, are ye now made perfect by the flesh?" (Gal. 3:1-3).

There are three words in this last question that we need to examine carefully to fully understand the secret Paul was talking about. The first is the word *perfect.* It means "to complete," "to finish," or "to fulfill." The second is the word *flesh.* It refers to human nature apart from God. It has reference here to attempting to bring our Christian life to its intended goal, to completion, to fulfillment in our own power or strength apart from God. The third word is the word *Spirit.* You will notice that the word *Spirit* is spelled with a capital *S.* When that is the case, it refers to the Holy Spirit. Who is the Holy Spirit? The Holy Spirit is God in you. God has revealed himself as three persons. He has revealed himself as Father, Son, and as Spirit. We cannot understand the God of the Bible unless we see him as all three of these in one. God is one God, but he has revealed himself in three persons.

So the Holy Spirit is the third person of the Trinity. I do not understand the Trinity. Someone has said, "If we deny the Trinity we will lose our souls; if we try to explain the Trinity we will lose our minds." While I do not understand the Trinity, I do know this: all that there is of God is in the Father; all that was ever seen of God is in the Son; and all that was ever felt of God is in the Holy Spirit. That's the Trinity.

Before his ascension into heaven, Jesus promised his disciples that when he went away another companion would come from God to walk with them, teach them, and be their helper. As Jesus had been the constant companion of the twelve apostles for the past three years—he had guided them, taught them, encouraged them, and strengthened them—now the Holy Spirit would come to do those things for them and for future disciples.

He assured them and us that we would not be left alone to face Satan and the world on our own strength. While he had been with them only a little while, the Holy Spirit would come to abide forever. While he had walked with them, the Holy Spirit would dwell in them. The Holy Spirit would be to them and to all believers in the future what he had been up until that time (John 14:16-18).

The Holy Spirit came on the Day of Pentecost, and he dwells with us and in us even now. Since the Holy Spirit has come, God has not been "up there" somewhere in heaven or "out there" somewhere in space. He is "in here" within our hearts and lives. The moment we put our faith and trust in Jesus Christ as Lord and Savior, the Holy Spirit takes up residence within us. If you are a Christian, he is in you now. He is our constant companion, our teacher, and our strength for victorious discipleship. The more we yield our lives to his control, the more we have the power for triumphant Christian living.

Paul's question again is this, "Are you so foolish? having begun in the Spirit, are ye now made perfect in the flesh?" We begin the Christian life in the Spirit. It is the Holy Spirit who convicts us of sin. It is the Holy Spirit who converts us to Christ. It is the Holy Spirit who adopts us into the family of God. It is the Spirit who guarantees our place in heaven. Wouldn't it be foolish to begin the Christian life in the power of the Holy Spirit and then attempt to complete it, finish it, bring it to its intended goal in our own strength by the flesh?

The obvious indication is that this would be foolish indeed. No person in his or her right mind would begin the Christian life by trusting in the grace of God through the Holy Spirit, then try to complete the Christian life by trusting in his own strength through the flesh.

Jack Taylor, in his best-selling book *The Key to Triumphant Living,* tells how that even as a minister he came to a point of almost complete frustration and exhaustion by trying to live the Christian life in his own strength. Jack wrote that after he became a Christian, no one told him about the Holy Spirit. So he thought that he had to live the Christian life on his own. His father was a farmer, a very good farmer.

Jack reasoned that if his father could become a good farmer by hard work, then he could become a good Christian in exactly the same way. So he worked with all of his might, almost to the point of total despair, to become a good Christian and a good minister. The end result was frustration and defeat. That's when he found the key to triumphant living. That key was and is the power of God's Spirit living in us.

Many of you have experienced the same frustration. You have tried to minister for Christ, and you have failed. You have tried to overcome bad habits and destructive attitudes, but you have been unable to do so. You are bored, moody, and unhappy. Though you want to change and have promised yourself a thousand times that you would, you have been powerless to do so. And you are destined to utter and complete failure as long as you continue in your own strength. Don't be so foolish as to try to bring your salvation to completeness by the flesh. You began the Christian life through the work of the Holy Spirit; now continue it through the same Holy Spirit, and you can know victory.

Since this is true, why do so many Christians live defeated and frustrated lives? There are at least three possible reasons. Sometimes it is because we are unaware of the indwelling of God's Spirit within us. Sometimes it is due to sinfulness. We are not walking in obedience after the Lord. Sometimes it is due to unbelief. We do not allow the Holy Spirit to flow through our lives. If your life is not a life of victory, then perhaps it is due to one of these three reasons.

Possess What You Own

Many people are living defeated Christian lives simply because they do not know about the power and the presence of the Holy Spirit within them. In Pecos County in West Texas, there is a famous oil field known as Yates Pool. It was called Yates Pool because the oil field was discovered on a sheep ranch that was owned by Mr. Ira Yates. During the depression years, Mr. Yates was not making enough on his ranch to pay the principle or the interest on his mortgage. It looked as though he might lose the ranch. He scarcely had enough money to buy food and clothing for his children, and like so many people in that day he lived off government relief. Many times he must have wondered where the next meal would come from and how he could continue to exist under those circumstances. One day a seismograph crew came through Pecos County and asked for permission to drill a wildcat well on his land. Mr. Yates signed the lease; they drilled the well, and at 1,115 feet they struck oil. The first oil well produced 80,000 barrels of oil a day. Then they began to sink more wells, some of them producing twice that much oil. In fact, thirty years later, a government test revealed that one of those wells was still capable of producing 1,025 barrels of oil a day. The amazing thing is that Mr. Yates owned it all—every bit of it. The day he bought the ranch, the oil and the mineral rights were his. But he was living on relief. He was a multimillionaire, but he was living in poverty, and the reason was that he did not know the oil was there. He owned it, but he did not possess it. He was ignorant of its existence; consequently, he lived his life in poverty until he discovered that resources were available to him.

In the same way, there are many Christians who live their lives in spiritual poverty instead of spiritual abundance because they do not know the power and the resources that are available to them through the Holy Spirit who dwells within them.

"But," you ask, "can a person be a Christian, and be indwelled by the Holy Spirit and not know about it?" They certainly can be. Paul wrote to the church at Corinth, "What? know ye not that your body is the temple of the Holy Ghost which is in you, which ye have of God, and you are not your own? For ye are bought with a price: therefore glorify God in your body, and in your spirit, which are God's" (1 Cor. 6:19-20).

Obviously, the Holy Spirit dwelt in these Corinthian Christians. Their body was his temple, but they were not fully aware of it. The Holy Spirit was in them, but they were ignorant of that fact; therefore, they lived their lives in the flesh.

In the course of his missionary journeys the apostle Paul encountered a brilliant, Alexandrian Jew by the name of Apollos. Apollos had been touched by the preaching of John the Baptist and was going about preaching and teaching the things of the Lord as he understood them. He had a tremendous grasp of the Scriptures, an energetic spirit, and he was an eloquent speaker. With great boldness he declared what he knew and believed concerning the Lord.

When Aquila and Priscilla, fellow missionaries of the apostle Paul, heard Apollos, they not only recognized his tremendous ability; but they also realized his deficiency in knowledge. Apollos did not know that the Savior that John the Baptist had predicted had already come. He did not know that the Lamb of God who had come to take away the sins of the world had already been slain. He didn't know that Jesus had been resurrected from the dead. He did not know that the one who would baptize with fire and the Holy Ghost had already done his work. Apollos was living in the New Testament era, but he had an Old Testament experience. So Aquila and Priscilla called him aside and taught him the whole truth concerning God, Christ, and the Holy Spirit.

I can imagine the response of Apollos as Aquila and Priscilla explained to him the whole gospel. He probably said, "What, do you mean that there is more to the Christian life than I have experienced?" And they must have said, "Yes, there is more, much more" (Acts 18:24-28). Apollos then accepted Jesus as his Savior and Lord, received the Holy Spirit, and began preaching with even greater power. Luke records that he "mightily" convinced the Jews and publicly showed by the Scriptures that Jesus was Christ (Acts 18:28).

Apollos now had power for even greater things in his life. Listen! Without the Holy Spirit your life may be spectacular, but it can never be miraculous. It is only the power of the Holy Spirit that can enable us to minister, live, and serve mightily. The key to triumphant living for all of us is the Holy Spirit of God who came to reside in us and to energize us the moment we became Christians.

What Kind of Person Are You?

The second reason why many Christians live defeated lives is unconfessed and unforsaken sin. They are not walking in obedience to Christ, and the Holy Spirit does not control their lives. The cleansed life is a prerequisite for a victorious life. God will not use or bless the lives of his people if they continue in their sins. We must repent of our sins, confess those sins, and begin to walk in obedience to the Lord if we want him to use us and to bless us.

There are three kinds of people in the world according to the apostle Paul. There are natural people, spiritual people, and carnal Christians. Everybody is one of these three kinds of people. The natural man (1 Cor. 2:14) is an unregenerate sinner. He is the man in his natural state spiritually. He has never received Jesus Christ as his Lord; he has never repented of his sins; he is not a Christian. He is lord of his own life. Christ is outside the circle of his experience. He is spiritually dead in sin. He is a man without God.

The spiritual man or woman (1 Cor. 2:15) is a person who has repented of sins and received Jesus Christ as Lord and Savior. Her sins are forgiven. She has been adopted into the family of God, and heaven is her home. She has

voluntarily abdicated the throne of her life, and she is allow-
ing Jesus Christ to rule her. She lives her life in conscious
fellowship with the Son of God and daily surrenders her life
to the lordship of Christ.

The carnal Christian (1 Cor. 3:3) is a Christian who continues to live his life in the flesh. The word *carnal* comes
from the same word that is translated "flesh" in Galatians
3:3. It refers to human nature apart from God. The carnal
Christian, then, is a person who once repented of his sins,
received Jesus as his Savior, and became one of God's children. But instead of living his life in the power of the Spirit,
he is once again trying to live it in his own strength., The
desires, appetites, and practices of the flesh now characterize his life.

When we are saved, we do not become puppets in the
hand of God. We still have a will of our own. Anytime we
want to, we can take control of our lives again. We can live
our lives in our own strength in the flesh, or we can live
them in the power of the Holy Spirit. The choice is always
ours.

The carnal Christian is a Christian who is seeking to live
the Christian life in her own strength. She no longer surrenders her life on a day-to-day basis to God. She tries by her
own efforts to live the Christian life.

The carnal Christian is the most miserable kind of person
there is. He is like the third of the three boys who were
going swimming one hot summer day. As they neared the
swimming hole one of them broke into a run, leaped up in
the air, grabbed his nose, and hit the water with a splash.
He began to swim around joyously. The second young man
followed close behind, but instead of jumping into the
water he stood right on the edge of the pond and began to
walk around the edge on dry ground. The third boy came
to the pond and started to wade very slowly out into the icy

water. His teeth chattered, and he shivered all over as he inched out into the deeper water.

The first boy was as happy as he could be. He was all the way in. The second boy was happy in a different way. He was all the way out. But the third boy was miserable because he was half in and half out. The higher the water got, the colder he became, and the more miserable he was.

Many Christians today are just like that. They are miserable because they are neither out nor in. They are halfway in between. They are Christians, but they do not know the victory that Jesus can give. They may be in the church every Sunday; they may teach a Sunday School class; they may sing in the choir; they may even stand in the pulpit. But their lives are not controlled by God's spirit; thus they are miserable, defeated, and frustrated.

Which kind of person are you? Are you a natural person? Are you a spiritual person? Are you a carnal Christian? You are one or the other. There are no other options. If you are not living a victorious Christian life, then in all probability it is because you are either a natural person or a carnal Christian. Yield your life to the Spirit of God today. Begin to obey him, and you can know the power for victorious living.

Don't Quench the Spirit

The third reason why many Christians are living defeated lives is the result of unbelief. Faith is the shaft that we sink deep down into the resources of God. Without faith, we can never know God's power for victorious discipleship. Faith opens the channel of God's blessings, so they can flow into us and through us. Unbelief shuts off God's power to our lives.

Paul warns, "Quench not the spirit" (1 Thess. 5:19). The word *quench* means "to extinguish," "suppress," or "inhibit." It is possible for us to hinder the working of the Holy

Spirit in our lives. Can you remember a time when you were washing your car and wanted to move the water hose? You did not want to go back to the faucet and cut the water off, so you simply bent the water hose together and clamped it with your fist. By this method you hindered or suppressed the flow of water through the hose. In the same way we can quench the flow of the Holy Spirit through our lives.

Nothing quenches the work of the Spirit like unbelief. And nothing releases the Spirit like faith. Did you know that you can do almost anything by faith? I mean anything! President Dwight D. Eisenhower once told about the Allied invasion of Europe during World War II called "Operation Overlord." He said, "From the beginning we knew that we were going to win. We didn't know it factually. We knew it by faith." I have heard of doing a lot of things by faith, but I had never heard of winning a military campaign in that way. What did he mean by "We knew it by faith?" He meant that they were so convinced that the victory was theirs that they launched an attack. They believed, therefore, they committed the troops to action. They claimed the victory by faith.

You and I claim the victory in Christian warfare the same way. By faith we believe that Christ is in us. By faith we yield our lives to him. By faith we act. And as we act, God works to accomplish what we believed in the first place. The secret to victorious living, then, is the spirit of God. It is, as Zechariah said, "Not by might, nor by power, but by my spirit, saith the Lord" (Zech. 4:6).

Are you sick and tired of being sick and tired? Are you discouraged and defeated and frustrated to the point of giving up? Then—wonderful! That's just where God wants you. Now that you know that you cannot live the Christian life on your own, perhaps you will allow God to do it in you and through you. The secret is to give up. It is to surrender. It is to let the spirit of God control your life.

Recently, I visited a prospect for our church, and as we talked I asked him to tell me about the time when he became a Christian. He said it happened two years before. He was going through a divorce and a financial crisis, and, he said, "I just bottomed out. So I got down on my knees and said, 'Lord, I can't do it. I can't go on. You've got to come into my life and take over.'" He said that when he did that he felt a peace and a release that he had never known before, and his whole life began to change.

That can happen to you also. Do not be so foolish as to begin the Christian life in the Spirit, then try to bring it to completion by the flesh. A disciple is one who daily yields his life to the Holy Spirit, so he can bring his Christian experience to completeness, to fulfillment, and to its intended end. That's the secret of Dynamic Discipleship.